The Pleasure of the Game

Best Wishes
From Aline

Mary McAleary

THE STORY OF THE TORONTO CRICKET, SKATING, AND CURLING CLUB, 1827-1977

Stanley Fillmore

The
Pleasure of
the
Game

Design: Frank Newfeld

TORONTO

CRICKET, SKATING, AND CURLING

CLUB

1977

ISBN 0-9690712-0-5

TORONTO CRICKET, SKATING
AND CURLING CLUB
141 Wilson Avenue
Toronto, Ontario M5M 3A3

ALBUM CONCEPT: FRANK NEWFELD

PRODUCTION, PRINTING & BINDING:
THE HUNTER ROSE COMPANY LTD.
TORONTO CANADA

ACKNOWLEDGEMENTS

I am indebted to a large number of people for their unstinted and enthusiastic sharing of knowledge about the three original clubs which
today constitute the Toronto Cricket, Skating, and Curling Club.
Without their help this book could not have been written. I cannot begin to name all who contributed their time and reminiscences. That
there were dozens more—hundreds more, perhaps—who might have
helped I have no doubt; I am sorry that time did not permit more to
have been contacted.

I gratefully acknowledge the help of the club's historical committee under the chairmanship of Tom Lutton; the committee responded
positively and promptly to every request for help. Mrs Mary Shaw was
everready with advice and assistance, especially in the early days when
I was groping about in new and unfamiliar territory. Bill Prentice was a
patient and gracious instructor in the finer points of cricket.

Norm Bracht was helpful in pointing out some of the more important but obscure research sources. Jim Bentley was a patient tutor ex-
plaining the finer points of racquet sports.

Tom Beattie, Peter Charles, Jack Dickinson, Andrew Dodge, Jack
Eastwood, Jim Galloway, Mrs Lois Harling, Harry Jackson, David Kennard, E.F. Loney, Kenneth MacDiarmid, Peter MacEwen, Alex Mackay, John Milsom, J.F. Moore, Errol Morson, Bert Northey, Trevor
Owen, Hap Philp, Guy Saunders, Mrs Kay Severs, Robert Suckling,
Martin Taylor, William C. Terry, and John W. Thompson gave their
time and their knowledge freely. I thank all of them.

I am uniquely indebted to George A. Thompson of the skating
section, who, on two occasions, helped me to see much more clearly a
number of details that had been obscure.

Two former members of the club, Fielding Biggar and James
"Sandy" McKechnie, also spent considerable time with me and I am
grateful.

At Upper Canada College I was greatly assisted by the efforts of
Roger Allen, Barbara A. Barrow, Harold Roberts, and Timothy Herron.

Bob Mackay of The Hunter Rose Company efficiently coordinated
the efforts of everyone involved and James Bruce pulled all the loose
ends together.

The manuscript was typed, *twice*, by Margaret Gray, a task that
commands my awe and gratitude.

Finally I should like to acknowledge the research assistance of Eileen Baker. Historical research is often boring, only occasionally exciting, and it demands in those who practise it a spirit of dogged inquisi-
tiveness. Eileen Baker possesses this spirit in large degree and she is
aware, I hope, of my grateful thanks.
S.F.

✳

*Among the early memorabilia preserved by members of the TCSCC, and gathered
for this publication, was a booklet printed in 1840. The Canadian Curler's
Manual was written by James Bicket, Secretary to the Toronto Curling Club.
In very poor condition, the original is believed to be the only copy. Because of its
Canadian character and archival interest it was considered important to preserve
it in some manner. A facsimile edition is inserted into the back flap of the jacket.*

Contents

For Pat

Opening of the Toronto Club Rink
by Lord Dufferin in 1877

ONTARIO

OFFICE OF

THE LIEUTENANT-GOVERNOR

QUEEN'S PARK

TORONTO

As the representative in Ontario of Her Majesty
The Queen, I am pleased to send my best wishes to the
Toronto Cricket Skating and Curling Club on its 150th
Anniversary.

I was intrigued to learn that one of my
predecessors, the Lieutenant-Governor of the day, Sir Francis
Bond Head, watched cricket matches of the Toronto Cricket Club
while sitting on his horse and often in the winter time attended
curling 'spiels.

Although it's not likely I will be visiting the Club
on horseback, I'm looking forward to attending the official
ceremonies marking the birthday 1827-1977.

The history of the Town of York, the City of Toronto
and the Province of Ontario is interwoven through the 150 years
of the Toronto Cricket Skating and Curling Club, and I'm most
pleased to offer my congratulations on your sesquicentennial.

Writing the history of the Club is a contribution
to everyone who appreciates our heritage and culture. May
I also offer best wishes and the best of sporting luck to all
who enjoy "The Pleasure of the Game".

Pauline M. McGibbon,
Lieutenant-Governor.

This they all with a joyful mind
Bear through life like a torch in flame,
And falling, fling to the host behind,
Play up! Play up! And play the game!

Sir Henry Newbolt

History in Canada has always been categorized as dull. This book is subtitled "The Story of the Toronto Cricket Club 1827 - 1977" and the one thing the author has attempted to do is to make it readable. I think he has done a remarkable job. Torontonians are no longer indifferent to the city's past and for this reason I think the book quite rightly dwells at length on the early days of the town of York, or early Toronto, when our club was just getting underway. We should be very proud of the fact that the origins of the club go back so far.

As a Torontonian born and bred, and a cricket enthusiast, I think it is important that Canadians realize that the most important summer game in this country for almost a century was what many still describe as the finest team game played. It is peculiar that curling, tennis, and lawn bowling, all played at the club today, are considered quite normal Canadian pastimes. Cricket, however, is still an "English" game and foreign to Canada, even though it is still played regularly in six of the ten Canadian provinces.

When our board of directors decided to celebrate the 150th anniversary of the club, one of the first decisions made was to have the club's history written. One of the directors, T.G. Lutton, was asked to mould a team to produce a suitable book. Mary Shaw and I, as co-chairmen of the committee, took the position that the history should be a professional work, even though such an undertaking is relatively expensive.

We must thank the Ministry of Culture and Recreation of the Province of Ontario for the grant which has been provided to help us defray the costs incurred. Also a vote of sincere thanks must be extended to Stanley Fillmore, the author of the book, who became caught up in the subject of Toronto's early history and the club's beginnings, and did more research and spent more time than we could reasonably expect. Our appreciation is also extended to Robert Mackay of Hunter Rose Company Limited, Toronto, the printers of the book. Bob prodded and pushed the untrained members of the committee and like the collie dog rounding up sheep in the Highlands, managed to keep the group pointed in the right direction.

The members of the committee constantly reminded one another throughout the writing of the book that our sole object was to produce a history that many people would want to read, rather than the usual dry tome of dates and events. We were aware that we would receive criticism, not so much for what the book contained, but for what it omitted. This first book could not possibly cover every colourful event, recount every memorable date, and recite all those treasured memories that add up to "the pleasure of the game". If the history kindles a flickering flame of pride that this unique Canadian club has survived to be passed along to our children, then the book has made the contribution that was intended.

William B. Prentice
MAY 1977

The history of any institution – sports club, political party, industrial complex – is inseparable from the history of its time. John Donne wrote, "No man is an island, entire of itself," and neither is the Toronto Cricket, Skating, and Curling Club. Its history is entwined in the life of Toronto from its earliest days. To completely tease apart the strands of history, to single out those threads that represent only the cricket, skating, and curling clubs is impossible, not to say undesirable.

To cite but one example: The Toronto Cricket Club was founded in 1827 by George Anthony Barber, among others. Barber and the others were masters at Upper Canada College. The college was founded largely through the efforts of one man, the Reverend (later Bishop) John Strachan. Had the Anglican church not posted Strachan to a York parish, Upper Canada College might have been established in Cornwall, from whence Strachan had come; the Upper Canada College masters would have formed the Cornwall Cricket Club. In any case, the TCSCC would be today a different organization than the one which celebrates its 150th anniversary.

In the pages that follow I have attempted to tell the stories of the three constituent clubs as concisely as possible while retaining enough of the supplemental material to indicate the place each club occupied within the life of the city itself.

One aspect of the combined histories which has suffered is the degree to which membership in the early clubs overlapped. John O. Heward was one of the earliest members to join the Toronto Cricket Club; he was also one of the first to join the Toronto Curling Club; a direct descendant was one of the Toronto Skating Club's presidents in the 1920s. William Dummer Powell, an attorney-general of Upper Canada in the early nineteenth century, was a benefactor of the cricket club – its first home grounds were situated on a corner of the racetrack located on his property. William Dummer Powell Jarvis, a direct descendant, was one of ten members of the Toronto Skating Club who died in action in the first world war, and whose sacrifices are remembered with a bronze plaque hung in the TCSCC.

The list goes on. Readers who are TCSCC members will know of many others – too many to include within one book's scope.

In the text of this book I have used contemporary street names to identify locations within Toronto. The older names – while in many cases interesting – were often changed and are capable of causing some confusion. Today's University Avenue used to be called College Avenue; to identify the cricket club's first grounds as located "near the corner of College Avenue and College Street" is unnecessarily distracting.

Editorial comments within quoted passages have been hedged with square brackets [ ]; in other places parentheses ( ) have been used.

Stanley Fillmore

TORONTO, MAY 1977

CHAPTER ONE

How it All Begin

Dawn, when it came, was only a slight improvement on the dark. Light came slowly, imperceptibly gliding from darkness to a half light. Snow was falling, tiny, globular pellets driven before a cutting wind. The temperature in those pre-Celsius days stood at twenty degrees Fahrenheit. It was Tuesday 13 March 1956 and it was a miserable, bitter morning.

J.A. "Sandy" McKechnie woke, rolled over, and glanced out the window. "Damn," he thought, "More damn snow." Then he remembered.

The events of last night, recalled in pleasure, softened the scowl on his face; the frown was replaced with something close to a smile. The snow, for the moment, didn't matter at all. McKechnie closed his eyes, stretched languidly, and returned to warm, happy sleep.

For McKechnie and eight companions, last night had been the climax of long months of hard work. The nine men constituted a committee composed of members of the Toronto Skating Club (of which McKechnie was a member) and the Toronto Cricket Club. The committee had worked for almost a year to put together a proposal for the amalgamation of the two clubs. Last night at a meeting of the skating club – the meeting held at the theatre of the Royal Ontario Museum because the turnout was too large to have been contained within the clubhouse – a majority of the members had voted overwhelming approval for the amalgamation plan put forward by the committee. It was the first major step in a plan that would rationalize the operations of both clubs, see them through a period of uncertain financing. McKechnie and his cohorts had ample reason to feel content.

Within the year – though no one could have predicted it on that March morning – a third club, the Toronto Curling Club, would join the partnership and the Toronto Cricket, Skating, and Curling Club of today would be born.

At the time, 1956-7, the reasons that the clubs were facing straitened finances seemed confused, complicated, intricately involved. With the passage of time the causes are more readily seen in their essentials.

All three clubs faced one paramount problem: Each was a one-season club. Each had bought property, erected a clubhouse, constructed playing surfaces. In every case, however, this large capital expenditure was fully utilized for, at most, six months of the year; the membership was, in effect, paying twelve-month dues for a half-year's use of the club.

The skating club from its headquarters at 568 Dupont Street faced another problem; it needed more space for the training of skaters. The problem had been almost constant. Starting in 1928, a scant seven years after the clubhouse had been built, the club had been forced to look for secondary ice surfaces where carnival productions could be rehearsed. The dimension of the problem can be appreciated when it is realized that often as many as 350 to 400 skaters took part in the carnivals and that rehearsals lasted for months right through carnival production in mid-March. In an article in *Maclean's* of 1938 a writer said,..."rehearsals start in the early winter and last from four o'clock until midnight, six days a week."

Obviously there was little time for training those skaters more interested in national or international competitions than in carnivals.

A third problem intruded on the skaters. When the clubhouse had been built on Dupont Street in 1921, the location was central for most members. In the meantime the city had grown, population had shifted. A survey of the membership showed that the majority lived *north* of St Clair Avenue.

Finally, the post-war popularity of professional ice shows was achieved at the cost of the TSC's carnival; audiences which had flocked to the carnival in earlier years avoided it now. Nonetheless, production costs had soared. The carnival was laid to rest—and with it went a significant source of the club's revenues. (In earlier years the club had survived a similar blow to its finances. When the clubhouse had been built, part of its operating costs had been covered by rental of the rink to the general public. That financial prop had been kicked out by the building of free, outdoor rinks by the city.)

While the skating club was struggling with its problems, the membership at the Armour Heights headquarters of the Toronto Cricket Club was facing a similar crisis, declining revenues, but for different reasons.

No matter how its devotees may have bemoaned the fact, cricket was not a popular sport in Canada. There was little or no encouragement of the sport in the Canadian public school system. Few colleges, apart from those with a close affiliation with the Anglican Church of Canada, fielded teams; and even there—as at Trinity College in Toronto—the shortening of the school year to September-May semesters had dampened enthusiasm for the sport. There was no organization in cricket to compare with the amateur hockey associations that guided a youngster's sporting steps from kindergarten to the eve of his professional debut.

In a word, the Toronto Cricket Club could not attain and sustain a membership sufficiently large to cover its yearly expenses.

Simultaneously, the Toronto Curling Club faced a problem uniquely its own: its clubhouse and property on Huron Street was about to be expropriated by the University of Toronto.

So in 1956-7 the three clubs had their problems. They also had certain assets—assets that were to be the salvation of all three of them.

The skating club (through the Winter Club) owned a valuable piece of midtown property and had a substantial bank account, thanks to several years of successful carnivals and an increasing membership.

The Toronto Cricket Club, though usually in a short cash position, sat upon some ten acres of property (some of it held on a long-term lease from Cricket Development Limited) in the prosperous and growing north end of the city. During the leanest years it survived by selling off lots on the periphery of its Wilson Avenue property. (Saunders Street, the north-south street to the east of the club's grounds, was built on land sold by the club and is named for Dyce W. Saunders, one of the club's mainstays in the late nineteenth century.)

The curling club, also, owned valuable property certain to bring a considerable price from the university, and the club also showed a sizeable bank balance.

The order of the names of the constituent clubs within the title of the new club was decided on the toss of a coin. Robert Suckling for the cricketers and Sandy McKechnie for the skaters flipped—Suckling won and chose to have the cricket club's name first. A year later when the curling club joined, its name was affixed to the end of the new club's name. Thus, the Toronto Cricket, Skating, and Curling Club.

The club was born in the middle years of the twentieth century. But its roots, its first activities, stretch back to the early years of the nineteenth century. York—as the city was then known—was a mere stripling when cricketers, skaters, and curlers first started to pursue their sports on the fields and ice of the settlement.

THE
Earliest Years

A young soldier, pushing his sweetheart on a bearskin-covered
sled, casts flirting eyes on one of another pair of skaters. This
romanticized scene was sketched in the artist's studio about
twenty years before the TCS was founded. It bears little relationship to skating as TSC members first knew it.

No century holds a monopoly on hi-jinks performed on ice

Burning off an excess of sheer animal energy, two soldiers *(left)* take their penny-farthing bicycles for a spin on a skating rink. On the frozen surface of Toronto Bay, families in two-horse cutters *(below)* and farmers with loads of firewood from the Island, find the ice strong enough to make an ideal thoroughfare. The drawing of the cyclists appeared in a Montreal periodical in 1881 and is a scene from Ottawa.
The watercolour of the Bay was probably done from life in 1835 by J.G. Howard, a surveyor and architect who designed Upper Canada College and who gave his home, High Park, to all future generations of Torontonians.

The two faces of the Bay

Abustle with the commerce of summertime, the wharves of Toronto's waterfront near the foot of Church Street reveal little of their wintry look when curlers appear in numbers.

Civilization reaches B.C.

British Columbia became a province in the early 1870s and even then cricket was being played in Beaconhill Park, Victoria *(above)*. A TCSCC team won top honours here in 1976.

Competitive XIs

Several times in the late 1800s, an English nobleman,
Lord Hawke, brought his personally-sponsored cricketers
to Canada. Here, he is shown *(standing fifth from left
in broad-striped blazer)* with his 1891 crew and an
Ottawa team. W.G. Grace's portrait *(opposite)* hangs in club.

Arch. S. Wortley

W.G. Grace

1890

The great thoroughfare of Toronto

When it published this engraving of Toronto's King Street in July 1880, the *Canadian Illustrated News* of Montreal called it the "great thoroughfare of Toronto." Then, the importance of the street was considerably greater than it is today; certainly it was closer to the waterfront through which much of Ontario's trade and commerce were funnelled. Since these early days Toronto's waterfront has inched steadily south as various landfill projects have been approved and completed.

Year 1890

How
to tell
a *true* curler

A curler – a *true* curler – will go to almost any extreme to
gratify his passion. These gentlemen *(above)* spent a considerable sum of
money and time to dam the Don River in the early 1800s and
thereby improve their curling surface. Their sons and grandsons
curled on indoor ice at the Huron Street site of the Toronto
Curling Club *(opposite top)* and may have commuted from suburban
homes in Seaton Village via the Spadina car line *(bottom)*.

There is always a vocal gallery

This sketch of a Toronto bonspiel was carried in a winter issue of the *Canadian Illustrated News* in 1875. It offers some consolation to present-day curlers: Even one hundred years ago the back lines were crowded with onlookers, each one insisting upon telling you how to play your rock. The French have a saying: "Everything changes and everything remains the same." It is as true of curling today as it was when these gentlemen (not a woman in sight) played their hearts out a century ago. The location is Lake Ontario in front of the present Canadian National Exhibition grounds. The buildings in the background are army barracks.

Cricket in Toronto
1891

For the first forty years of its existence as an English settlement, Toronto – or York, as it was soon christened – suffered under the label of "Little," or "Muddy York". Little it certainly was. As originally laid out the town site stretched from the waterfront north only to Queen Street; its eastern limit was Parliament Street, its western limit Peter Street. And muddy? At the best of times, with weeks of sunshine drying the streets, the dirt roads were pocked with mudholes; the village was surrounded and laced through with swampy patches of ground that never thoroughly dried.

A few stores, and the occasional private residence, were dressed up with a few yards of plank sidewalk but, by and large, York gentlemen and ladies hoisted trouser legs and skirts over their boot tops and sloshed through the gumbo. Galloping horses and speeding carriages bespattered the unwary.

John Graves Simcoe planted York in 1793 on the site of the old French garrison, Fort Rouillé. He admired the harbour and considered the location defensible against the newly liberated colonies of the United States.

York was second best, in Simcoe's mind, as a capital for Upper Canada; he preferred "Georgina-upon-Thames," the inland setting of the present city of London. The Governor General, Lord Dorchester, vetoed Simcoe's first choice and by default Toronto became the capital of Ontario.

Within months of his initial landing, Simcoe, a dedicated, lifelong monarchist, changed the Indian name of Toronto to York in honour of the royal family. It wasn't a new habit – Simcoe had been busy renaming sites long before he founded York. A traveller of those early days, Isaac Weld, complained about Simcoe's policy: "It is to be lamented that the Indian names, so grand and sonorous, should ever be changed for others. Newark, Kingston, York are poor substitutes for the original names of the respective places Niagara, Cataraqui, Toronto." York it remained for forty years.

York was a garrison – some 200 officers and men of the Queen's Rangers comprised the majority of the townspeople and the fort, at the foot of today's Bathurst Street, represented the largest collection of buildings. Slowly, the town grew. Government increased in size and complexity; the presence of significant numbers of bureaucrats created a demand for service trades – wheelwrights, saddlers, tanners, blacksmiths, merchants.

As the settlement grew, so grew the demand for supplies and services. Taverns and inns were among the first to sprout; within a few years – in the early 1800s – when the population of the town remained fewer than 900 persons, some forty taverns were scattered along every street and avenue. They were drinking spots, surely, but more than that; in the bursting growth of the new settlement they were community centres as well. Politics was their lifeblood, spirituous liquors merely lubricants. It was in such a tavern, the Sun at the corner of Queen and Yonge Streets, that William Lyon Mackenzie rallied the members of his Reform Party; and it was from another, Montgomery's on Yonge Street just

CHAPTER TWO

It Was Aptly Called 'Muddy York'

This view of Toronto was drawn some
time after 1834, a few years after George
Barber arrived in the city. The scene
looks east along King Street to the
corner of Church. On the *extreme left* is
the courthouse; the church with the tall
spire is St James.

north of Eglinton Avenue, that Mackenzie's supporters sallied forth in their aborted rebellion of 1837.

Other signs of a growing community were soon in evidence. In 1815 the town contained but seventeen shops and seven storehouses, but the assessment rolls of 1833 listed more than one hundred. The first St James Church had been built (on the same site the cathedral occupies today at Church and King Streets) and the 1833-4 city directory lists the following church-related groups operating in the town: the York Auxiliary Bible Society, the African Chapel ("Established for the Religious Worship of colored people"), the Society for Promoting Christian Knowledge, the Upper Canada Religious Tract and Book Society, the Missionary Society of the St Andrew's Scotch Church in Canada, the Missionary Society of the Methodist Episcopal Church in Canada, the York Branch of the Canada Auxiliary Wesleyan Missionary Society, the Missionary Society of the Upper Canada Primitive Methodists, the Society for Converting and Civilizing the Indians and Propagating the Gospel Among the Destitute Settlers in Upper Canada, the Society for the General Relief and Benefit of Strangers and the Distressed Poor of York, and the Upper Canada Temperance Society.

By the 1820s, settlers in large numbers began to swell the town's ranks; the Napoleonic wars in Europe were concluded and British immigrants, crowded at home, flooded to Canada. In the twenty-five years between 1805 and 1830 the population of York grew from fewer than 500 souls to almost 3,000.

The newcomers required supplies and a sizeable market. Coincidentally, merchants in the town, with some governmental assistance, had established the Bank of Upper Canada and had incorporated an insurance company, both ventures supported financially with local capital. The town's foundations were well and truly laid. So solidly was the settlement planted that when the capital was moved to Kingston in 1841, the city (by then incorporated as Toronto) suffered no diminishment of its vitality when the government and its personnel transferred to the new site.

A growing civilian population meant increasing numbers of small children; early in the city's history, schools were established for the education of the young. One of the first (in 1807) was the Home District or Royal Grammar School, located on the block between Richmond and Adelaide Streets, midway between Jarvis and Church. (The Home District was an administrative area, one of four in Upper Canada, that was centred on Niagara and which included York within its boundaries.) The grammar school was what we would call a combined primary-secondary school, insistent that its students be thoroughly grounded in the classics. It was, for a time, the closest thing the colony possessed to the great public schools of England where the sons of well-placed gentlemen were schooled in social graces as well as the classical disciplines.

To the Home District School in 1825 came a young teacher from England, George Anthony Barber. Barber was to leave his mark on the educational, sporting, and business life of York and Toronto.

G.A. Barber arrived in York in the company of the Reverend Dr Thomas Phillips, of Queen's College, Cambridge, newly appointed as

The Reverend Dr Thomas Phillips, an agreeable and outgoing scholar of the classics, was a Cambridge graduate who was named principal of York's grammar school. He brought Barber with him and thus, unwittingly, planted the seed of the Toronto Cricket Club.

headmaster at the grammar school. Phillips was an affable man whose good nature easily encompassed the often rude pranks practised by small boys in all ages. He was a traditionalist in many ways; Dr Henry Scadding, a pioneer historian of the city and himself a student under Dr Phillips's instruction, wrote of his teacher: "He was a venerable-looking man – the very ideal, outwardly, of an English country parson of an old type . . . The costume in which he always appeared (shovel-hat included), was that usually assumed by the senior clergy of some years ago. He also wore powder in the hair except when in mourning. According to the standards of the day, Dr Phillips was an accomplished scholar, and a good reader and writer of English." Phillips taught Latin and Greek as well as English and, so much a perfectionist was he that his students translated Greek into – not English but – Latin.

Barber's specialities were mathematics and writing – penmanship as we would call it. They were twin talents that would see Barber through a lifetime. For several years, in the forties, he was the editor, and then

George Anthony Barber served a long and useful life in the affairs of the city. This portrait, not dated but presumably from his middle years, shows him as a mature individual, much as he must have looked during his proprietorship of the Toronto *Herald*.

publisher-editor, of the weekly *Herald,* one of the first Toronto newspapers to carry regular news of sports. Over the years almost every civic meeting concerned with the cost of street lighting or road paving was served by G.A. Barber as secretary. He further used his penmanship as secretary of the Toronto Turf Club for several seasons. And as late as 1856 Barber was drawing a salary from the city for his work as a municipal auditor.

From all accounts Barber was a calm, even-tempered man. One account which mentions him as a cricket instructor says he was "patience itself" while teaching the game to youngsters. T.D. Phillipps called Barber "a thoughtful tutor and kind foster-parent in cricket." The only instance recorded of Barber speaking with passion is the editorial he wrote for the issue of the *Herald* dated 22 June 1848.

The publisher of this Journal [Barber wrote about himself] is under the unpleasant necessity of announcing, that unless other arrange-

Among his many other interests, vocations, and enthusiasms, George A. Barber was an inverterate collector of cricket bats, particularly those he had wielded in matches to which he attached particular importance. During his life, and while he was still active as a cricketer, his collection amounted to more than sixty bats, we are told by a contemporary. Barber donated one of his bats to Upper Canada College where it is still on display. Timothy Herron, of the school's 1977 graduating year, shows the bat with Barber's name, fading with time but still legible.

ments should be effected in the meantime, the publication of the *Herald,* at the termination of the current half-year, will be discontinued – *for the simple reason only, that those who are indebted to the office will not pay their accounts with anything like regularity.* [Italics in original.] Appeals, humiliating to one's self respect to be compelled to resort to, for payment of arrears, many of three, and four years standing, have, from time to time, been made through the columns of this paper, but without much success – and had we been asking an alms, like a sturdy beggar, the result could hardly have been less satisfactory...if no arrangement to continue the paper be effected between now and the 1st July, the *Herald* will, however reluctantly, have to bid farewell to the Conservative party.

Barber's public life was amply covered in the press of the day.

Although he was a modest man – some said self effacing – his comings and goings were often detailed in his own newspaper, not in the editorial columns alone but in advertisements as well, where "G.A. Barber, Secretary pro tem" or "G.A. Barber, clerk," signed public notices. His private life was another matter. We seldom read anything of his wife or family. Not directly, that is. However, cricket scores from the 1850s on show the name of "G.A. Barber Jr" as a regular member of various Toronto elevens. On 17 August 1853, for instance, the Toronto club played "Yonge Street," Toronto winning in two innings by 143 runs. G.A. Barber scored 11 and 4 and G.A. Barber Jr made 11 and 16. (In the same game John O. Heward, a man whose name will recur many times in subsequent pages, made 7 and 13.)

Barber's most noteworthy characteristic, from our point of view, was his fascination with cricket; it was an addiction, a lifelong appetite that was satiated by neither repetition nor advancing age.

Barber's attachment to cricket was easily satisfied in York. When he arrived at the Home District Grammar School, a cricket ground was already in place. Who built it, and when, we have no clue. But Barber didn't question his good fortune. As soon as he felt that he had his classes under control, his lessons planned in advance, he was out on the field instructing his students in the subtleties of the game. Every day in season the schoolyard rang with boyish shouts of encouragement and derision as each player learned to bowl, keep wicket, field, and bat.

Without doubt Barber's classes produced at least twenty-two players – he would have been restlessly unhappy had his constant practices not yielded a real game once in a while. That he sought other teams as well, to test his team's mettle, we may be sure. No record exists to confirm either the fact of such games or their scores. But, with a reliable source of young, teachable talent, and with a ready-made cricket ground at his command, Barber would not have been satisfied to play pick-up games year in and year out.

Who would the grammar school team have played? The military team – or teams – for one.

Through the early years of York's history, several regiments of British troops were in barracks, first at the Old Fort and later in a new location to the west, on the grounds of the present Canadian National Exhibition. The officers and many of the ranks were cricketers from their earliest years in England; Donald King, for many years executive secretary of the Canadian Cricket Association, claims that the British soldiers in Montreal were playing cricket as early as 1795; their fellows-in-arms at York would not have been much behind. Certainly, within a few years, and within the span of recorded cricket history, military teams were in regular competition, and individual cricketers from the barracks were regularly added to bolster the ranks of civilian teams. It is perfectly logical to suggest that Barber's senior boys challenged the military teams on many occasions.

Today, in the waning years of the twentieth century, it sounds strange to our ears to suggest that military cricket teams and civilian teams may have worked and played in close cooperation. In the early years of the last century, however, the military presence was an obvious, necessary, and important part of every civilian's life. For one thing, the soldiers constituted the largest single category of the population—there were more soldiers in York, for example, than there were English civilians in the first years. Later, well into the middle years of the nineteenth century, the garrison remained a pivot of Toronto social life and its soldiers were notable contributors to its various activities. G.G.S. Lindsey, an outstanding member of the club in the latter years of the nineteenth century, wrote of cricket at Upper Canada College that for ten years, "between 1860 and 1870, thanks to the kindness of the officers of the garrison, the soldiers were allowed to come to the school and coach the boys. The officers themselves, among them Captain Willoughby Wallace, a former captain at Harrow, . . . materially bettered the form of the boys."

Barber's cricketers? He would have recruited the best players from among his senior students, of course. But in addition, who would his cricketers have been? They came from the town itself, young men and some who were no longer young, some recent immigrants from Britain and some who had been in town for a number of years.

Some residents, too old, too stiff, or too disinterested to play themselves, encouraged their sons; the Honourable Chief Justice, John Beverley Robinson, did *not* play, so far as we know, but his namesake, young J.B. Jr, did. W.H. Boulton, another justice in Upper Canada and Ontario, later served for some ten years as president of the Toronto Cricket Club but was not, himself, a cricketer; his sons were. Finally, Barber would have tapped a constantly growing source of trained talent—his own graduates.

Cricket was not the sole sport played in early York.

*   *   *

Scots were among the earliest settlers at York and they brought with them their unbounded enthusiasm for the national game of curling. Within a few years dedicated bands of curlers were clearing the ice on Toronto Bay for use as curling sheets. For curlers—and for skaters, as well—Toronto Bay was an ideal location in the days before covered rinks; Toronto Island, or the Peninsula as it was known before a storm in the

Credit for being the first Canadian cricket team to visit England is usually awarded to "George Lindsey's eleven," a team organized by Lindsey of the Toronto club and captained by Dr E.R. Ogden and which included Dyce Saunders on its roster. The team played various English clubs in 1887. The honour is misplaced, however. The first Canadian team played in England in 1880 and suffered a series of disasters, on and off the field, that most cricket historians prefer to forget. Among other problems was the fact that the team captain, one Trooper Dale, a deserter from the Royal Horse Guards, was arrested on the field and hauled off to court martial. He was sentenced to one month's imprisonment, escaped, was recaptured and sentenced anew to a full year. The team abandoned the tour half completed, and slunk home.

The penetrating odours of hot tar and gutted fish hang over the docks of Toronto. This scene was sketched about 1840 by the English travel artist, W. H. Bartlett. Beyond these wharves, when winter had frozen the lake surface, early members of the Toronto Curling Club played their favourite game.

mid-nineteenth century ripped out the eastern land connection, provided a well-treed windbreak. In the lee of commercial loading docks located on the waterfront between Bay and Church Streets, York's curling and skating contingents practised. In the early 1830s, John G. Howard, a local architect and surveyor who bequeathed his estate to the city as High Park, sketched in water colours the gaiety of the skating scene.

In 1827 Dr John Strachan, the Anglican archdeacon of York and a citizen of awesome energies, received royal assent from England for the establishment of a university in the town. Some years before, he had convinced the colonial administrators to set aside the block between John and Simcoe, King and Adelaide Streets as a college reserve. However, when his plans became known, the sectarian nature of the proposed college was vigorously criticized and Strachan faced mounting opposition in the province. The arrival of a new lieutenant-governor, Sir John Colborne, was the final blow to Strachan's plans. Colborne halted all progress on the proposed university and instead took over the King Street site for the establishment of a new preparatory school – Upper Canada College.

The new school was merged with Dr Phillips's Home District Grammar School at the beginning, and for the first year of its existence used the Home District School building between Jarvis and Church Streets. Later, when UCC assumed a separate identity, the former grammar school continued to function as a municipally-funded secondary school and eventually metamorphosed into Jarvis Collegiate.

The Reverend Dr Phillips, principal of the grammar school, was named vice-principal of Upper Canada College. (The principal was the Reverend Dr James H. Harris, a fellow of Clare Hall, Cambridge, and a brother-in-law of Sir John Colborne, lieutenant-general of Upper Canada.) George Barber was named a master of writing and mathematics, and carried another responsibility as "collector" of the college, or registrar.

Upper Canada College opened its doors to students on 8 January 1830 but it was not until the following year that students and masters moved to the new buildings. By then, the main school building, a solid, two-storey structure in red brick, and four houses for boarders and masters—also in red brick—had been completed. Also ready was the cricket pitch, which occupied the western end of the campus.

The school went on to produce uncounted numbers of superior athletes, cricketers to be sure, but outstanding performers in *all* sports. One of the first—and a graduate of the cricket pitch—was John O. Heward. In a unique tribute to Heward, the Reverend T.D. Phillipps, one of the giants of early Canadian cricket, wrote:

> ...my dear old friend J.O. Heward was the life of the College eleven. No pluckier or luckier batsman ever handled the willow. And the two characteristics, luck and pluck, complements of good, nervy play, are mighty factors in the compilation of heavy scores, which Jack had more to his credit than any other...

Much later, in June 1851, a Toronto newspaper carried this challenge:

> Eleven gentlemen, Canadian born, or who have learned the game in Canada, renew their challenge of last year—to play a match at cricket against "Old Country" gentlemen—to come off on the Toronto club ground, Monday, July 28th, 1851, or on any other day that may be mutually agreed upon.
>
> (On behalf of the "Canada" Eleven), Toronto, June 28th, 1851.
>
> JOHN O. HEWARD.

By 1830, York had grown to considerable proportions. The town's population stood at 2,860 souls and three years later had leaped to 6,094. Suburbs had sprung up—Yorkville, York Mills, Weston, Thornhill were attracting settlers in increasing numbers. The town's growing prosperity did not occur in isolation; the whole colony of Upper Canada was growing—from 177,174 persons in 1827 to 321,145 in 1834. York was the central town in this growing land, the location from which the agricultural produce was shipped, and the source of retail and wholesale merchandise required by the growing population.

Simcoe's military engineers had broken trail through the province with Yonge Street running north and south, and Dundas Street threading together the settlements from east to west. Since the earliest days, a program of road building continued to push new routes through the bush. York was well embarked on its career as a metropolis.

By 1842, York, or Toronto as it had been renamed, made a strong impression on a sophisticated visitor from Britain. Charles Dickens, ever alert for the ironies of life and position with which he filled his novels, found Toronto a lively city:

> ...We emerged on Lake Ontario [from the Niagara River], an inland sea; and by half-past six o'clock were at Toronto.

JOHN STRACHAN

JOHN O. HEWARD

41

The country round this town being very flat, is bare of scenic interest; but the town itself is full of life and motion, bustle, business, and improvement. The streets are well paved, and lighted with gas; the houses are large and good; the shops excellent. Many of them have a display of goods in their windows, such as may be seen in thriving country towns in England; and there are some which would do no discredit to the metropolis itself. There is a good stone prison here; and there are, beside, a handsome church, a court-house, public offices, many commodious private residences, and a government observatory for noting and recording the magnetic variations. In the College of Upper Canada, which is one of the public establishments of the city, a sound education in every department of polite learning can be had, at a very moderate expense: the annual charge for the instruction of each pupil, not exceeding nine pounds sterling. It has pretty good endowments in the way of land, and is a valuable and useful institution.

The first stone of a new college [King's College, predecessor of the University of Toronto] had been laid but a few days, by the Governor General. It will be a handsome, spacious edifice, approached by a long avenue, which is already planted and made available as a public walk. The town is well adapted for wholesome exercise at all seasons, for the footways in the thoroughfares which lie beyond the principal street, are planked like floors, and kept in very good and clean repair.

Dickens's only complaint about the city was the violence of its politics:

It is a matter of deep regret that political differences should have run high in this place, and led to most discreditable and disgraceful results. It is not long since guns were discharged from a window in this town at the successful candidates in an election, and the coachman of one of them was actually shot in the body, though not dangerously wounded. But one man was killed on the same occasion; and from the very window whence he received his death, the very flag which shielded his murderer (not only in the commission of his crime, but from its consequences), was displayed again on the occasion of the public ceremony performed by the Governor General, to which I have just adverted.

In the middle years of the nineteenth century, Upper Canada and Toronto were caught up in the great era of steam locomotion. In England, and on the continent, railways had become almost commonplace. In the United States, the hustle-bustle and entrepreneurs had rammed roads through to every corner of the original colonies, and had thrown lines out to the frontiers of the territories. Travellers returning to Upper Canada from a journey abroad were agog with the new marvels.

The fever had originally flared up in the thirties; the first road in Upper Canada was built in 1839 and connected Queenston and Chippawa as a portage around Niagara Falls. But the grades on the line were too steep for the locomotives of the day and for years the trains were pulled by horses. In 1845, a traveller on the line wrote, "You are whirled along, not by steam, but by three trotting horses at a rapid rate through a

wood road till you reach the Falls." In 1854 the line was rebuilt to connect Chippawa and Niagara-on-the-Lake and at the same time it was converted to steam.

Also in 1854, through the subscriptions of private citizens in the town of Cobourg, the Cobourg and Peterborough Railroad began operation. The original plan had been to transport lumber and produce from the inland site of Peterborough to the lake port of Cobourg. For a time it worked; Cobourg boomed, its port became one the busiest on the Great Lakes.

Mismanagement and some unscrupulous profit-taking reduced the line to bankruptcy, although it continued in intermittent service until the first world war, when its tracks were uprooted and shipped to France for use on roadbeds built to transport ammunition.

As early as 1837 Toronto was *hoping* for a railway. In May of that year city council granted to the Lake Huron Rail Road Company ownership of certain waterfront lots for the construction of warehouses. It led, not to the immediate construction of the railway nor to warehouses either, but to a movement that eventually saw the whole of the Toronto bay front owned by private rail companies.

The Mackenzie rebellion of 1837 coincided with an economic depression to throw a pall over the province and a recession, fatal to railways plans, followed.

It was 1853 before a steam locomotive actually chugged its way out of Toronto. It was an engine of the Ontario and Simcoe Huron Union Railroad destined for Aurora. In seven short years more than "300 locomotives were thundering and bellowing" over lines in Ontario, wrote T.C. Keefer, a Toronto engineer who built many of the lines and who, in his time, was a distinguished cricketer with the Toronto Cricket Club.

When finished and ready for students, Upper Canada College consisted of a large, central building in which most classes were held, and four smaller buildings used primarily as residences for masters and students. The college was located on the north side of King Street west of today's University Avenue. The sketch is by John G. Howard, the school's architect.

43

The St. Mary-le-bone Cricket Club (the MCC as it is known today) is the mother club of cricketers everywhere. It used this illustration to decorate the first page of its book, *The LAWS of the NOBLE GAME of CRICKET.*

The primary motive for the railway builders had been the trade – commercial trade – the trains would carry. Human passengers had been considered, but barely. Still, it was from the human passengers' point of view that the most dramatic change took place when the railways entered the life of Upper Canada.

In the first place the pell-mell stampede to build the roads plunged almost every municipality in the province deeply into debt. In the ten years between 1851 and 1861 the towns, cities, and counties of Canada West borrowed more than $6.5 million from the Municipal Loan Fund for railway construction; in the same ten years the *default* on interest alone amounted to $2.7 million. Some 1,400 miles of road were built in the province.

Even more important, in the long run, was the way the railroads extended the world of the colonists. Friends and relatives living more than a few miles distant were no longer virtually inaccessible. Montreal was no longer a week away by stage coach or steamer but a mere day's travel – a tiring day, to be sure, but a saving in time that bordered on the miraculous.

As early as 1834, when the Toronto Cricket Club started playing a series of matches with the Guelph Cricket Club, the teams had to meet on neutral territory at Hamilton because the distance from home base to home base was too great to be adequately managed in reasonable travelling time. Even then the Toronto eleven required four days for a match: a day travelling by stage coach to Hamilton, two afternoons of play, and another day returning to Toronto.

For Toronto, and for other settlements located along the Great Lakes, the steamers had been an alternative to the roads. In 1846, for example, when the Cobourg cricket team visited Bowmanville for a match, the Cobourg cricketers travelled aboard the steamer *America* although the distance traversed was but twenty-five miles.

Indeed, some travellers preferred the steamers even after the railways were well established and convenient to use. Mrs Edward Copleston, an English immigrant, described with great affection her steamer trip from Montreal to Kingston.

These vessels, at first sight, seem little better than huge, floating hotels; but are admirably adapted for the miscellaneous traffic they carry on; for not only are they capable of stowing away several hundred passengers, but hundreds of all kinds of live stock besides. These last occupy the lower deck, while the passengers are comfortably ensconced on the upper, and the remainder of the vessel has great capacity for general merchandise. Anything better suited for family travel would be difficult to suggest; with plenty of room for promenade on deck, a luxurious drawing-room, supplied with piano, newspapers, and books – an excellent *table d'hôte*, and capacious and separate berths (dignified with the name of "state-rooms").

Onward you glide, enjoying the lovely scenery of the St. Lawrence; no time lost by day or night, and all this quite free from the fatigue, or weary monotony of railway travel...

Mrs Copleston's jibes at railway travel were not far from the mark. The trains were noisy, bouncy, dirty. Dickens, on the same trip mentioned above, grumped unhappily: "There is a great deal of jolting, a great deal of noise, a great deal of wall, not much window, a locomotive engine, a shriek, and a bell."

One's fellow travellers were apt to be boors and the railway employees were often not much better. Charles Richard Weld, a British travel writer, described a typical journey after a vacation trip through Canada and the United States in the fifties of the nineteenth century:

> The American railway car ... is about forty feet long, eight and a half wide, and six and a half high, having seats, with reversible backs, for sixty passengers. The weight of a car of these dimensions is eleven tons. . . . It is supported at each end on four wheeled trucks, ingeniously mounted on swivel axles, enabling it to whish round curves at the sight of which an English railway engineer would stand aghast. The locomotive is very unlike ours, being an uncouth-looking machine, with a prodigious bottle-nose chimney, and an iron-barred visor-like affair in front, called a cow-catcher ... the American engine differs also in its interior economy from our locomotive, feeding on wood, for which it has an insatiable appetite, instead of coal, which may account for the unearthly sound it emits, comparable only to the simultaneous braying of a dozen donkeys labouring under oppressive asthma. A conductor, unmarked by any badge of distinction beyond a small plate, which he only displays when the train is in motion, ... shouts to the engine-driver, "all o'board;" a bell, attached to the engine, is rung violently, not to summon indolent or tardy passengers "on board," for they are supposed to be in the cars – but to warn people in the streets of the approach of the locomotive, and the train is off. . . .
>
> The rate of travelling is about twenty-four miles an hour. The stoppages are frequent, to take in wood, which burns more rapidly than coke. At these wooding stations, unfortunate horses may have been seen toiling up an endless incline, which retrogrades beneath their feet, and sets machinery in motion to saw logs for the locomotives.

Finally, in 1856, the Grand Trunk Railway connecting Toronto and Montreal was opened and a new era of cooperation, social, and business intercourse opened. The Grand Trunk snaked its way west, too, and by 1859 stretched all the way to Sarnia. One of the most noted contractors on the Toronto-Sarnia stretch of road was the Toronto engineer C.S. (later Sir Casimir) Gzowski whose family was later to play a large part in the affairs of the Toronto Skating Club.

Though he had been impressed with Toronto, author Charles Dickens didn't think much of the "wide, open spaces" of North America as he observed them from the windows of a moving train.

> ... the road is very narrow, and the view, when there is a deep cutting, by no means extensive. When there is not, the character of the scenery is always the same. Mile after mile of stunted trees: some hewn down by the axe, some blown down by the wind, some half

fallen and resting on their neighbours, many mere logs half hidden in the swamp, others mouldered away to spongy chips.... Now you emerge for a few brief minutes on an open country, glittering with some bright lake or pool, broad as many an English river, but so small here that it scarcely has a name; now catch hasty glimpses of a distant town, with its clean white houses and their cool piazza... when whir-r-r! almost before you have seen them, comes the dark screen: the stunted trees, the stumps, the logs, the stagnant water.

As valuable as they were in expanding the horizons of Toronto businessmen, the railways were of equal or greater value extending the scope of the Toronto Cricket and the Toronto Curling Clubs. By the time the railways became an accepted part of everyday life in the early sixties, both clubs had been in existence for more than twenty years. Playing members of each club had tested their strength against all the local and neighbouring opposition. Even in the earliest years the curlers had established firm rivalries with other distant clubs in Fergus, Galt, Hamilton, Guelph, Niagara, and even as far as Kingston. In every case an out-of-town game stretched into a three-day affair, a good deal of the time spent lugging about one's personal stones often weighing as much as eighty pounds apiece. Bonspiels were an expensive, time-consuming, and exhausting business.

Regular trains, running on reasonably predictable schedules, took much of the dreariness out of the games. Toronto cricketers and curlers could now entrain for Belleville, play a game, and be home again in less time than they had previously needed for a game in nearby Hamilton.

The additional competition was good for both clubs. With limited competition, no matter how good, one's standards of play are based on restricted tests of competence. The railways offered the chance of expanding the horizons of competitiveness in both cricket and curling clubs, and the clubs responded with superior play and innovative tactics.

In a later age it was the creation of the Canadian Pacific Railway that provided the visible strand tying together the scattered settlements that John A. Macdonald and his parliamentary confreres insisted upon calling a nation. In a lesser way, the earlier construction of the Grand Trunk and the smaller lines was a unifying force in the two Canadas. Certainly it was the roads of steel that helped create a unity of purpose, a shared sense of destiny.

With all the other benefits of superior communication came a metamorphosis that transformed the Toronto Cricket Club and the Toronto Curling Club into sports bodies of more than local importance—they became national organizations. Neighbourhood concerns gave way to broader interests. In but a few years each was to become a truly international organization.

"Having, during my sojourn... passed... up and down the most of Canada West, and part of Canada East, I had sufficient experience of the railways to enable me to state definitely my opinion as to the comparative comfort of travelling in that country and our own.

"So far as I could judge, their railways are not so well built, nor yet kept in such good repair as ours....

"But if their railways be more rickety than ours, as a general rule, their 'cars', as they call them, are as much superior to ours in comfort as a drawing-room is to a shepherd's cottage."

GEORGE EASTON
Travels in America

46

ACTION ON THE PITCH

R.B. BLAKE

In 1872, the Toronto Cricket Club played host to a touring English XII captained
by R.A. Fitzgerald. The best known cricketer to accompany the team was W.G. Grace,
a batsman of legendary prowess. The thought of catching him out or
of bowling him out must have inspired the dreams of TCC members. R.B. Blake,
Toronto's first bowler had his photograph taken to commemorate his participation.

1872

The Match

The Reverend T.D. Phillipps was an early stalwart of Canadian cricket. He played most often with St Catharines but occasionally brought his bat to Toronto's aid.

The famous game in which W.G. Grace batted against the Toronto club took place on the Taddle grounds which T.D. Phillipps (*opposite*) had called the best in North America. By

this time Toronto had grown to a respectable size and was assuming her place as one of the commercial and manufacturing centres of the new dominion. In this drawing of the match the new buildings of the University of Toronto decorate the background with University College and the Croft Chapter House shown on the right. Some professors, marked with academic caps, mingle with the players of both teams. Grace is shown at the left wicket, his bat lowered in readiness. R.B. Blake (*in black hat*) is about to begin bowling.

1874

The Reverend T.D. Phillipps (*seated, extreme left*) tried several times to organize Canadian teams to tour England. This "all-Canada" team was not one–this occasion was a "tourney" in Halifax– but by 1880 Phillipps had organized an English tour; a series of disasters, on and off the field, sent the team home in disgrace.

1887

Touring Canadians (several from the TCC) and their English hosts pose for a group portrait in England. The setting is not identified but appears to be a covered patio or porch of a hotel, or ale house.

1887

Canadians pose again with yet another of the teams they met in England on the 1887 tour. Canada was slow entering international competitions—the International Series excepted—but once initiated she responded promptly and aggressively to all challenges.

1891

The Toronto Cricket Club seldom lacked opponents but when a free Sunday afternoon occurred, the members chose up sides and played an intramural game. The two teams, seniors all except for the junior sprawled in front, gave themselves names of old Hebrew tribes.

1910

Audaciously labelling themselves the Canadian Zingari, these intrepid cricketers set forth on an English tour in 1910. The experience was to provide Norman Seagram (*this page, lower right*) with his first taste of transatlantic competition and convince him of the necessity of testing the club's skills against other than just local competitors. Seagram's dedication to the club was a positive force in the early years of the twentieth century; the mark of his personality was indelibly impressed on the Toronto Cricket Club and on the TCSCC that followed.

May 28, 1910.

CANADIAN CRICKETERS
The Zingari Eleven Which Plays Seve

film reversed!

Pete was right handed!

H. G. DAVIDSON.

A. H. GIBSON.

G. N. Sh
C. J.
A. Gillespie   R. C.

A. A. BEEMER.

G. H. SOUTHAM.

N. SEAGRAM.

AVING FOR TOUR OF ENGLAND

atches in Great Britain, Opening at Liverpool on June 30

N GENTLEMEN IN ENGLAND, 1887.

W. J. Perry   L Ogden   G. G. S. Lindsey   Dyce W. Saunders
W. Jose   W. A Henry   W. W. Vickers   R. B. Ferrie
Ogden   Arthur C Allan   W. C. Little   W. L. M. Lindsey

W. W. WRIGHT.

S. R. SAUNDERS.

P. E. HENDERSON.

W. J. FLEURY.

W. S. GREENING.

H. F. LOUNSBOROUGH.

1910

Seagram (*seated second from right*) brought his left-handed bowling and his reliable bat to the aid of the Canadian Zingari on its English tour of 1910.

1922

In 1922 Seagram (*middle, front row*) assembled and financed his own touring team.

1926

During the mid-1920s, Seagram was a popular choice as club captain. Here (*in middle of row wearing cap*) he poses with the team that met the visiting Philadelphians in 1926. The building in the background is the former clubhouse the day it was opened.

1937

By 1937, with the second world war lurking unseen in the future, this all-Canadian team, assembled by the Hon R.C. Mathews (*middle of front row*), defeated the touring MCC by ten wickets. Seven of the twelve were Torontonians–Derby Loney sits on Mr Mathews's left hand.

1939

This summer, war was just around the corner. In less than a year the membership had dwindled as members entered the services and more than one club family had felt the sting of wartime death. All three clubs went into what one member called "wakeful hibernation".

1964

In this year, a touring Yorkshire XI met TCSCC eleven for two days running. In the first innings (*below*) Vince Taylor (*left*) and Ted Wigley sprawl in an attempt to spear a Yorkshire hit. *Opposite*, Ali Kahn of Toronto gets a hit but it seems Vic Walker is run out.

1964

The junior XI (*right*) and the single-wicket contestants (*below*) were part of the club's contingent at a "cricket day" held in September at King City, Ontario. Many of these youths have gone on to more adult awards at the club and in sports in general.

1969

This TCSCC cricket team was the first overseas private club to play the MCC at Lord's; rain cancelled the play. Len Maile (*bottom*), Toronto captain, receives consolations from Dennis Compton after TCSCC team lost to Middlesex second eleven during the same 1969 tour.

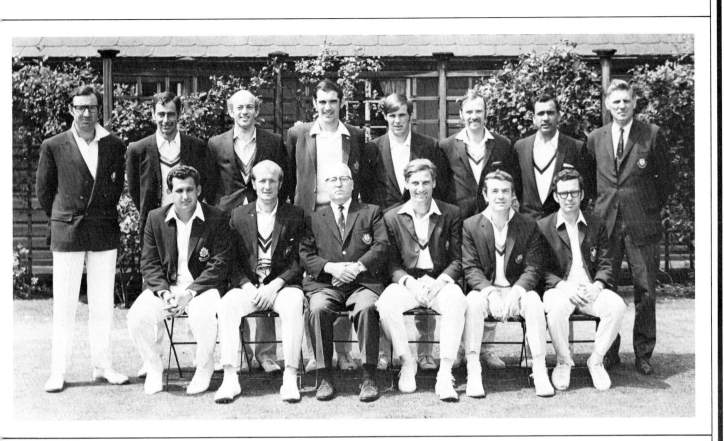

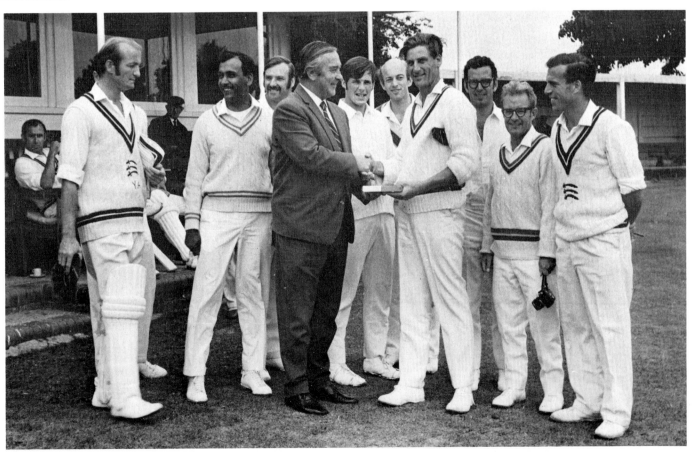

1970

In this year, the Australian Emus toured Canada and provided many citizens with their first look at cricket as it is "played down under." For still more Canadians, it was the first glimpse ever of *any* kind of cricket—the match at the club was the first ever produced on national television. In photos *below* and *opposite* TV cameras may be seen lurking in the background. The Toronto team lines up (*bottom*) in an "attacking field," anticipating a ball hit to one side; eight of Toronto's eleven may be seen clustered behind the batter. From the left the players are John Harvey, (John Rowe, the batter, faces Ric Stevens, bowler, not seen), Ali Kahn, Basil Peters, Tony Clarke, Mark Foster, Ron Aldridge, Roger Rayson, Achal Moorjan

115

1976

Practice
and practise:
In moments of
depression, a
cricket player
often thinks
his life, his
world, his
universe is
bounded by
this noun,
practice, and
this verb,
practise.
If he is
diligent,
however, and
not too
rebellious,
the practice
and the
practising
eventually
pay off.
For proof,
see *below.*

1976

Tony Clarke's
(he is *seated,
third from left*)
team invaded
Vancouver
Island in
September of
1976 and
returned with
proof that it
was the best
cricket team in
Canada–the
John Ross
Robertson
Trophy. Debbie
Aldridge was
the team's
scorer and her
presence was
a welcome
injection of
feminine charm.

I t is Wednesday, a warm day in May. The sun, high in a spring-blue sky, is almost an hour past its zenith. In the topmost branches of the elm and oak trees a slight breeze rustles the leaves. Below, on the ground, it is still and mild. Off in one corner of the field, two bowlers warm up, pitching in turn to a wicketkeeper. Around the periphery of the field the members of both teams congregate in small groups, two, three apiece. A crowd of perhaps two hundred persons has gathered, some civilian, some military, some men, some women, a few children, all festive.

Somewhere in the distance a church bell rings once; one o'clock. The umpires stride onto the field and take up their positions. They are followed by the players in disorganized ranks. A batsman stations himself at each wicket, a bowler steps into place, the fielding team distributes itself about the field. One umpire calls, "Play!" The second repeats the instruction, "Play!" The game is underway.

The teams are well matched – in apparel, at least. One team, the military at field, is clad every man in white: trousers neatly pressed, unmarked this early in the game by grass stains, long-sleeved pullovers in white wool with blue and red bands picked out in the cuffs, white shoes, white caps.

The two batsmen, representative of the whole team, the balance of which lounges about the sidelines, wear whites also but without the overall effect of a uniform. Their trousers are "white", as neatly pressed as their opponents, but not wholly matched in colour. The white shirt each wears open at the neck is cut to the owner's preference, full in the sleeve, perhaps tapered at the waist. The player's individuality is expressed in his headgear; each sports a hat, chosen, it would seem, for its novelty. One a stovepipe topper, one a soft-crowned beaver. The hat remains perched atop its owner's skull, even while he's batting.

The dapper gentlemen in matched whites are officers and ranks of the 32nd Regiment of the British army stationed at the Toronto Garrison. The oddly-hatted crew is the first team of the Toronto Cricket Club, on its way to another victory on its home grounds of the Taddle.

It is 1842.

*   *   *

The history of cricket in Toronto – indeed in Canada – is long but shadowy. The predominance of the British presence in Canada has been an unchallenged fact (with only the exception of 1812 to prove the rule) from 1759 to the present. And wherever the British presence has been established, anywhere in the world, there also cricket has flourished.

So it was, doubtless, in Canada. But no written record remains. What little we know of cricket's early history is but an outline of events.

Still, much of the study of history is a search for logical explanations for gaps in the official record. It has been said that the study of history is similar to working a jigsaw puzzle and the analogy is a good one. A puzzle is usually worked from the outside in, from the outline to the centre. The outline is simplest to find. Once in place, it determines the shape, size, colour, and pattern of the piece that fits next. When you

CHAPTER THREE

Cricket Follows the Union Jack

63

One of the earliest sketches of York
shows the village in 1804, only eleven
short years after Lieutenant-Governor
John Graves Simcoe had established the
site as his capital. The sketch, a watercolour by Elizabeth Frances Hale, shows
the waterfront west from the fort which
is on the *extreme right* with the flag
flying high.

work at a puzzle you have an amazingly accurate picture in your mind of the piece you seek.

So it is with history: A certain period of time may be a blank, a hole. And still the events surrounding it impose certain conditions and define what could have happened. It is in this sense of logical problem solving that we approach the early history of cricket.

Toronto had existed for uncounted years as a campground for wandering Indian tribes before the first Europeans established a trading post on the location in 1749. The first settlement was French and was named Fort Rouillé in honour of the French colonial minister, Antoine Louis Rouillé, the Count de Jouy. The fort remained a small and insignificant part of the French fur trading empire for almost ten years; in the summer of 1759 the French fired the fort and left it in charred ruins when a British force, approaching by boats from Niagara, hove to offshore.

The site remained vacant—or, rather, returned to its original purpose as an Indian meeting place. A few itinerant fur traders settled briefly before resuming their restless wanderings. It was not until 1793 when Colonel John Graves Simcoe, governor of Upper Canada, put ashore near the foot of today's Bathurst Street, that the fortunes of Toronto picked up. Simcoe's engineers cleared a good-sized site and trimmed back the new growth on 300 acres previously cleared by the French.

Simcoe left York, as he rechristened the place, in 1796 and nothing in the record suggests that cricket was played during his tenure as governor. It is likely that the work of establishing the military fort and the civilian centre of government so completely occupied the soldiers and civilians alike that little time was left for recreation. Certainly, a full day's work swinging a broadaxe clearing land for a garrison hardly leaves a man eager to put in more hours pulling stumps for a cricket pitch. But the time eventually came when the garrison was fully built, the outlying blockhouses constructed and manned, the safety of the fort secured. Then, leisure hours—and, perhaps in the case of the enlisted ranks, some of the working hours, too—were spent levelling an adequate cricket ground.

Precisely when and where the cricket grounds were built nobody knows, but that they were built we may be sure; a few short years later, officers at the garrison were largely responsible for the construction of a horseracing oval on the banks of the Humber, on part of the grounds of what is today the Lambton Golf and Country Club. The track, small though it must have been, would have been a vastly more ambitious project than creation of a cricket ground.

At the same time the gentlemen officers of the garrison were building a pitch, civilian cricketers were probably at work as well. In the earliest years, the military personnel of York outnumbered the civilian population. But the village proper grew slowly, settled in large part by loyalists who had emigrated from the newly independent United States, but with increasingly large numbers of British nationals as well. At some point, the proportion of civilians slid past the military complement. From that point on, the English merchants, doctors, lawyers, surveyors, clergymen, and other professionals must have been playing cricket or cudgelling their brains for inspiration on where to build the field.

Speculation aside, by 1825 a cricket field had been built in York and it was maintained as a going concern. As we have seen, the field was incorporated as part of the grounds of the Home District Grammar School.

Once again, details are annoyingly absent. In a book published in 1893, George Dickson and Adam Mercer note:

> The ground surrounding the school which, in primitive times, was slightly undulating, had been cleared of the stumps, and a space for a few hundred feet square, was selected for the good old English sport of cricket, which was cultivated from 1825, under the enthusiastic direction of Mr. George Anthony Barber, who accompanied Dr. Thomas Phillips to York as his principal assistant in the school, and who was well known as the father of cricket in old Upper Canada.

GEORGE A. BARBER

Barber was, in truth, far more than just the father of cricket in Canada. He was midwife, patron saint, lucky charm, team founder, captain, instructor, promoter—he was a one-man cricket committee of enormous vitality, inexhaustible enthusiasm, and bottomless optimism. It is not idle speculation to suggest that had George A. Barber not existed, the Toronto Cricket, Skating, and Curling Club would be today a very different organization than it finds itself. Certainly it was Barber's determined presence that saw the club over its first few shaky years; it was Barber who provided the necessary incentive and continuity to cement the loose, informal group together.

Further, Barber was an organizer, an executive in today's terms. He delighted in imposing order upon chaos. In everything the man undertook, his orderly mind pushed, pulled, and kneaded the circumstances into a logical, sequential order. It is completely within character that he should formalize the cricket scene in York-Toronto with a club which, through its bylaws, could regulate play, arrange matches, discipline infractions.

(As we shall see, members of the Toronto Curling Club in 1840 published a booklet which, for the first time in North America, committed the rules of the game to paper. It is curious that the Toronto cricketers did not perceive a similar need for written rules and fill it, but no such guide was written. One was planned, however. In the 8 April 1844 issue of the Toronto *Herald*, the newspaper of which George Barber was then editor and later publisher, carried a one-column advertisement which read: "Cricket. Preparing for the press, and will be published early in the season, say, on or about St. George's Day, the *Cricketers' Hand Book*, Price 2s. 6d. by a member of the 'Toronto Club.' Toronto, MDCCCXLIV." No further mention is ever made to the book. The honour of being the first cricket book published in North America went to the *Canadian Cricketer's Guide* of 1857 edited by T.D. Phillipps of the St Catharines club.)

When the facts concerning George Barber and cricket are added up, the sum appears: Where Barber is on the scene, there cricket will shortly appear. If Barber lived in York in 1825, as we have seen, then cricket must have... We return to this theme within a few pages.

* * *

By 1831 the new buildings of Upper Canada College were completed on the King Street site, and the faculty and students moved to the new campus. Barber, of course, made the move and was joined by some five other masters who had arrived from England with the principal, the Reverend Dr J.H. Harris. Within a year or so, three more masters joined the staff, three whose names are second only to Barber's in the honour roll of early cricket in Toronto: the Reverend William Boulton, John Kent, and the Reverend F.W. Barron.

Boulton was the son of W.H. Boulton, son himself of one of York's first citizens and, in later years, mayor of Toronto for two terms. Young Boulton taught classics and had developed a taste for cricket while studying at Queen's College, Oxford. He died as a young man in 1834.

Little is known about Kent except that he was master of the UCC prep school and a devotee of cricket.

Frederick Barron joined the staff of UCC in 1834 as a classics master and was appointed principal in 1843. Barron's name is inseparable from cricket; it was Barber's genius for organization that established cricket at UCC; it was Barron's tenacity that nursed the young sport to the full flower it achieved and retained at the school.

By 1834 Barber, Barron, and Boulton had constructed a strong team of cricketers, the three masters themselves prominent members of the team, others recruited from the ranks of students and citizens. The eleven were playing under a name – the Toronto Cricket Club.

Two years later, in 1836, Barber, Barron, and Kent helped organize the Upper Canada College team and during July of that year took on the Toronto eleven. The masters solved the dilemma of the dual loyalty by playing with the students. Without the services of Barber, Barron, and Kent, the senior club lost the match. The *Patriot* reported the event in these words:

JOHN KENT

> National amusements are emblematic of national character; they partly borrow their tone from it, and partly contribute to form it. The fiery, restless Arab, delights in the tournament of the Jereed; the indolent, sententious Turk, strokes his beard. and with the chess board before him, whiles away hours without the movement of a muscle; the revengeful, stormy-souled Spaniard, gazes with a savage glee on the dying struggles of the bleeding Bull, and watches with a thrill of pleasure the risks and dangers encountered by the agile Matador. The ENGLISHMAN's game is CRICKET. It is a pastime dear to the London nobleman, and the Sussex peasant, – to the full-blooded youthful aristocrat of Eton; and the honest ploughboy of Hampshire. The players' virtues in this game are promptitude, activity, cheerfulness, and noiseless vigilance. "Still as the breeze, dreadful as the storm," is every combatant. On himself each deems the fate of the contest to hang; and so long as there is hope, and that is as long as the game lasts, each bears up with pluck against adverse tide of affairs. How fully, then, are the noblest traits of the English character manifested in this game! Cool courage, that does not spirt out at intervals but runs on with even tenor; animation without bluster; and action with but few words. If an occasional exclamation escapes the

lips of a bowler, or some vivacious players, it is as short and pithy as the Duke of Wellington's "Up Guards! and at them!"—or His present Gracious Majesty's "Go it, Ned." The green sward is the battle ground; and gnarled, patrician oaks, look down upon the scene with sombre complacency, little dreaming that their planks perchance will be trodden at no remote period by the striplings before them. The amusements thus carried on, amid the loveliest scenes of nature, and during the brightest, sunniest hours of summer, leaves an influence on the mind no less strengthening and wholesome than on the braced and invigorated body.

Such being our opinion of the surpassing excellence and virtues of cricket, we are delighted to hear that the boys of U.C. College have formed a cricket club. The members consist of some of the masters, ex-pupils, and boys at present pursuing their studies. The following are the officers:-

Patron	– His Excellency Sir F.B. Head
President	– Mr. Kent
Vice-President	– Mr. Lukin Robinson
Treasurer	– Augustus Keefer
Secretary	– Larratt Smith

Sir John Colborne always took the deepest interest in the promotion of this noble game and our present thoroughly English Lieutenant Governor is too accurate an observer of human nature, not to know that the amusements of the youth tinge the character of the man, and that British feelings cannot flow into the breasts of our Canadian boys, thro' a more delightful or untainted channel, than that of British sports. A cricketer as a matter of course *detests democracy & is staunch in allegiance to his King*. [Emphasis in original.]

The young cricketers, anxious to flesh their maiden weapons, challenged the Toronto Club on condition that *White*, a Sussex man, should be one of their eleven. The gauntlet thus thrown down, was quickly taken up; and on Thursday the match was played as follows:

TORONTO			
First Innings		*Second Innings*	
Draper, *b* White	0	*c* White	8
Murray, *not out*	9	*b* Barron	0
Lane, *b* Barron	0	*b* White	0
Nash, *stumped* Phillpotts	0	*run out*	2
Loring, *c* Barber	0	*c* Kent	2
Boulton, *b* White	7	*b* Barron	4
Head, *b* White	0	*c* Barron	3
Rowsell, *b* Barron	0	*b* White	1
Maddox, *b* Barron	1	*b* Barron	0
Humphrey's, *b* White	0	*b* Barron	0
Wakefield, *run out*	0	*not out*	1
Byes	2	*Byes*	4
			25
Totals	19		
Total of 2 Innings	44		

First Innings

White, *c* Head	6
L. Robinson, *b* Lane	7
Phillpots, *b* Lane	0
Kent, *b* Draper	7
A. Keefer, *b* Lane	0
Barber, *struck out*	0
J. Robinson, *b* Draper	7
Barron, *b* Draper	18
Dyett, *c* Boulton	0
Hale, *not out*	2
T. Keefer, *b* Draper	3
byes &c	10
	60
TORONTO,	
total of 2 Innings	44
	16

Won by the college, by 16 runs in One Inning, the Toronto men sustaining a defeat as complete as that which has recently overtaken those wretched animals yclept radicals. To the uninitiated, it may be necessary to state that *b* means bowled out, – and *c* caught out.

There was some excellent bowling, batting, and fielding on both sides. The day was brilliant, and the heat greatly tempered by a cool breeze. Several ladies sat under the trees, encouraging the players, and stirring them to emulation by their presence; and the respectable groups of spectators gazed on the animated spectacle with pleasure. At the conclusion of the match, His Excellency Sir Francis Head, rode up to the ground and was received with those clear-toned and hearty cheers, which the lungs of cricketers can so melodiously emit.

May the young Gentlemen of the College, *play* their *game* on the *field* of life, with a credit equal to that they have earned on Thursday, and may they never have to contend with opponents less generous than those whom they encountered on that occasion and by whom it would have been an honour to be defeated! Many of our Englishmen, heroes, lawyers, & divines, have, at the game of cricket, won youthful laurels, prophetic of those which overshadowed their maturer brows.

* * *

There has been – and still is – a great deal of discussion about the age of the oldest constituent club, the Toronto Cricket Club. Almost all histories of early Toronto list 1834 as the founding date. The club itself, in a preamble to the bylaws, supports the date of 1827, but the club letterhead, in use throughout 1976, carried the line, "Toronto Cricket Club (1832)". Which is correct? Which is false?

The bad news first.

It stretches the imagination too far to believe that the Toronto Cricket Club was founded in either 1827 or 1832. Toronto, as a place name, did not exist in 1827 or 1832, having been abolished in favour of York by Colonel Simcoe himself. That the name, Toronto, remained a favourite with residents is amply evident. But it flies in the face of logic to assume that Barber, John Beverley Robinson Jr, Strachan and others, all with close and intimate attachments to the Family Compact, should discard the royal name York for the Indian name Toronto.

True, *a* cricket club might have been formed – indeed, *was* formed – in 1827 but it would have been called the York Cricket Club, or the Gentlemen of York, or some similar name. When York changed its name to Toronto, the club did also and the TCC can legitimately trace its beginning to the founding of the earlier club.

George Barber arrived in York and started teaching cricket (among other things) to schoolboys in 1825. But building a school team takes time; Barber, at the same time, would have found himself surrounded by adults, mostly Englishmen like himself, who were already skilled cricketers. While Barber trained his schoolboys with patience, he undoubtedly assembled teams of adults to challenge the several military teams that stood by in the garrison ready, willing, and able to play.

Sometime in 1827 Barber and his adult cohorts organized themselves into a club, the York Cricket Club or whatever. They produced some kind of document – a constitution, bylaws, who knows? It may have been nothing more than a pledge that signatories would meet once a week to play cricket.

In 1834 the town of York became the city of Toronto and William Lyon Mackenzie became the city's first mayor. The resumption of the traditional name and the elevation to a city's status prompted parades, testimonial dinners, public presentations, balls, parties, social events of every size and description. Every organization, from the city itself to the lowliest knitting circle, met to celebrate the double event. If the organization's name had included the word York, a major ceremony marked the change of name.

So it would have been with Barber and his fellow cricketers. And so, quite naturally, 1834 would appear in most histories as the date on which the Toronto Cricket Club was founded. In a strictly literal sense, the histories are correct; in the broader sense of attempting to understand what happened, they are wrong by at least seven years.

Sometime after the meeting in 1827 at which the York Cricket Club was organized, the pertinent document came to rest with someone who recognized its importance and determined to store it safely. That the person was successful is evident from the fact that one hundred years later, in 1927, when the bylaws of the club were rewritten, the original document was cited as evidence that 1927 marked the one hundredth anniversary of the club. By this date, of course, the club was well established on its Wilson Avenue property.

The original document remained at the club, "safely stored" for all but exceptional purposes, until late afternoon on a day in March, 1952.

On that day a fire broke out in the attic of the club and before it was quenched some $37,000 damage had been done. Rather, the insurance company paid out $37,000 to repair the building; it was impossible to place a dollar value on the loss of the original document. It and several cartons of early records went up in smoke.

A thorough check of documents that remain, combined with a careful assessment of other historians' conclusions, leads inescapably to the fact the the Toronto Cricket Club (as the York Cricket Club or whatever) was founded *no later than 1827*.

The interesting speculation is what might have happened in the two years between 1825 when George Barber arrived in York and 1827 when he helped found the club? It can be said with certainty that if he wasn't organizing clubs he was at least organizing games.

The possibility remains that the TCSCC is older by as much as two years than the club claims. New discoveries of old documents are always being made. It is possible that a basement or an attic, a library or an archive, may yet yield papers to prove or disprove the possibility.

In 1836, the new parliament building and government offices looked like this. (The first, on Parliament Street, had been burned by US forces in the war of 1812.) The buildings were situated on the north side of Front Street at the corner of today's University Avenue. At the *right corner* of the buildings can be seen the steeple of St James Church on Church and King Streets, and on the *extreme right* is a glimpse of Toronto Bay with a sail.

The cricket pitch at Hamilton, Canada West, as Ontario was known in pre-Confederation 1863. The teams shown are not identified but a local club is probably represented. It was on this pitch that the Toronto Cricket Club established its early rivalry with the Guelph club some thirty and more years before the picture was taken.

The Toronto club played its first game – rather, the first game that found its way into the permanent records – in 1834. It was also the club's first out-of-town match; the opposition was Guelph and the two teams met on neutral grounds at Hamilton. In an age when all travel by land was on horse or foot, the seventy-mile trip between Guelph and Toronto was too great to be comfortably included in a two-day period. It is possible the Toronto team journeyed to Hamilton by lake.

The only surviving record of the match describes it:

> Guelph went to bat, and play was commenced by E. Thompson and White, whose wickets, with but four runs, soon fell to Lanes' bowling. Wilson and W. Thompson stood up next, and after displaying very fine and steady batting, and adding the former ten and the latter seventeen runs to the score, had their wickets lowered by A. Beeston.

Barnard commenced his innings with strong play, and, dashing out boldly and safely, had scored thirty-one runs when caught out.

Lane caught Murton the first ball, and Nicholls, who batted beautifully, went out for nineteen runs. Total of the innings, 102.

Guelph won the match 102 and 7 to Toronto 74 and 34. No details are given of Toronto's innings.

One of the Toronto players was John Beverley Robinson, Jr, son of the Honourable Mr Justice Robinson, chief justice of Upper Canada. In later years the younger Robinson recalled that he had been but thirteen years old, a student at Upper Canada College, when the game was played. It was, he said, the first game in Canada that took place between teams located at some distance from each other.

Despite the final score the game must have satisfied the Toronto club, for on 15 August 1835, it was back on the same Hamilton grounds, facing the same opposition. Toronto batted first; the scoring follows:

TORONTO

First Innings		Second Innings	
Draper, b Thompson	0	not out	0
Beeston, E. b Thompson	0	b White	3
Lane, c White	6	b White	6
Beeston, A. hit wicket	19	run out	15
Nash, c Thompson	12	c Thompson	1
Loring, stumped, Murton	1	c Barnard	1
Gwynne, c Thompson	0	b White	0
Illingworth, c Thompson	4	b Thompson	2
Barber, not out	19	c Wilson	2
Barron, b White	3	b Barnard	2
Boulton, b Barnard	4		0
Extras	6		5
Totals	74		37

GUELPH

First Innings		Second Innings	
White, b Lane	0	not out	4
Thompson, E. run out	8	not out	3
Thompson, W. c Nash	8		
Wilson, not out	48		
Barnard, b Lane	13		
Murton, c Draper	11		
Penfold, c Boulton	6		
Strouts, b Lane	0		
Nicholas, b A. Beeston	2		
Poore, b A. Beeston	6		
Neeve, c Loring	2		
Extras	4		
Total	108	Total for no wickets 7	

WILLIAM H. DRAPER

FREDERICK W. BARRON

Draper, who opened for Toronto, was William Henry Draper, a thirty-three-year-old lawyer of Toronto who was in a few years to distinguish himself as member of the legislature and as solicitor-general of the province. His son, Frank C. Draper, was Toronto's chief of police in 1874-86.

The "Three B's"—Barber, Barron, and Boulton (another son of W.H.—young William had died the year before)—are prominent in the line up. Robinson did not play, although the young man's cricket days were far from over.

Wilson, whose destructive bat was the main reason Toronto lost the match, was John Combe Wilson, one of four cricketing brothers, the most famous of whom was Sir Archdale Wilson who was to defend Lucknow in the Indian mutiny of 1857. John Wilson was a masterful player; an early writer described him as, "...one of the best bats of his time, hitting principally to the off between point and cover-point, and in the slips; and also a free hitter to long leg; he kept wicket sometimes, and was such an enthusiastic cricketer that he continued playing after one of his lungs had become perfectly useless."

A return match was arranged for 24 September of the same year and Toronto again lost—by 65 and 47 to 104 and 82. The Toronto complement remained largely the same as in the previous game; young John B. Robinson played (1 and 1 not out), John Kent, UCC master had been added to the team, and Henry Rowsell, lately arrived in Toronto, was a new team member. Rowsell, a member of the MCC in London, had just founded his King Street printing and publishing house, later to become a major force in the literary life of the province.

In 1836, largely through the efforts of Kent with a strong assist from Barber and Barron, Upper Canada College fielded its own team as already described. Its first match, with the TCC, was a rout for the members of the Toronto club. The *Patriot's* account makes no mention of where the game was played, but it was likely on the UCC grounds, which probably served as home base for both teams.

Sometime in the late 1830s or early 1840s, a combination of circumstances provided the Toronto Cricket Club with the first grounds it could call its own.

When John Graves Simcoe first designated York as his capital, the northern limits of the village were staked out at Queen Street. North of Queen Street, Simcoe laid out long, narrow lots of 100 acres apiece which were deeded to members of his government. These lots, some 660 feet in frontage by 6,600 feet in depth, stretched from Queen north to College Street. During the next twenty-five years or so, the ownership of many of these "park lots" changed by means of inheritance, sale, outright deeding.

The park lot at the corner of University Avenue and Queen Street was originally deeded to the Honourable William Dummer Powell, justice in the Court of King's Bench and later chief justice of the province. Powell built a large—and, for the time—rather lavish home on the estate and named it in Gaelic, Caer (Castle) Howell.

Next to Powell's estate to the west came D'Arcy Boulton's property on which his home, The Grange, was constructed. Boulton, one of the first judges appointed in York, was the father of W.H. Boulton and grandfather of young William, the UCC master. In the early years of the nineteenth century Boulton added to his holdings until he owned most of the property stretching from Powell's lot west to what is now Beverley Street.

In the meantime, young York sporting bloods who missed the excitement of horseracing in England, laid out several rough racecourses at various locations around the town. In 1837 a more permanent track was built on the banks of the Humber River on the estate of John Scarlett. The Runnymede track, known after the name of Scarlett's domain, was used for three years. At the time it closed – in 1840 – another track, grandly called the St Leger Race Course after the track of the same name in England, was opened on the Boulton property in Toronto.

By this time the Boulton estate had passed by inheritance to W.H. Boulton, D'Arcy's son. W.H. was a fan of racing, no doubt, but he was also a devotee of cricket. In the northeast corner of the track, at what is now McCaul and College Streets, Boulton set aside a corner of the tract, outside the second turn, for the exclusive use of the cricket club. There, at the Taddle, as the grounds were christened after the creek nearby, the Toronto Cricket Club was "at home" until later in the century.

Sometime after the cricket club was established on the Boulton estate, the Powell property to the east passed into other hands; the chief justice's grand home was remodelled and added to as a resort hotel, still under the Powell name of Caer Howell. Located at the corner of University Avenue and College Street, it was considered to be a fair distance from the city proper, and the wealthier families of Toronto frequented it as a resort, spending an afternoon at tea and conversation, or a weekend retreating from the business world.

In front of the hotel, and adjacent to the cricket pitch, were a bowling green and a sunken tennis court, reputedly the first in North America. While there was no formal association between the bowling, racquet sports, and cricket, it was, nonetheless, the beginnings of close physical associations that have persisted to this day.

The cricket club members erected a tent – a marquee probably donated by the military – as a clubhouse but it was used primarily as a changing room only. Tea for the midgame break was served by maids from the Caer Howell Hotel; postgame refreshments of sterner stripe were also available at the hotel.

(In the halls of the TCSCC today hangs a drawing of the famous match of September 1872 against England in which W.G. Grace appeared. In the background of the drawing, across College Street from the Taddle grounds, appear the outlines of some of the first buildings erected on the University of Toronto downtown campus.)

Wherever he played W.G. Grace was invariably honoured at dinner and almost inevitably toasted afterward in some overblown fashion – "the Champion Batsman of All Cricketdom" – that must have embarrassed him. Throughout he retained his good humour and sense of proportion. To a fulsome toast in his honour at Toronto in 1872 he replied briefly, "Gentlemen, I beg to thank you for the honour you have done me; I have never seen better bowling than I have seen today, and I hope to see as good wherever I go."

*   *   *

The Caer Howell Hotel, where the union of cricket, tennis, and bowling first flowered, was well into its decline when this photograph was taken. The photographer did not date his picture but it appears to be early twentieth century; the building was demolished in 1915. At its peak the hotel was a centre of Toronto social life, the focus of much activity in cricket, bowling, tennis.

Most books on the subject of cricket give 1859 as the date of the first international match. The books are in error.

The first match of a truly international character took place in Toronto in 1840 between teams of the Toronto Cricket Club and the St George's Club of New York. That the first game resulted from a hoax matters not at all. In spite of the unorthodox beginning, it led later to a long (although interrupted) series between Canada and the US that continues even today. (It should be noted that the US-Canada International Series does *not* recognize the 1840 game as the series' first; that honour goes to the next game in 1844, see p. 79.)

On the afternoon of 28 August 1840, eighteen members of the St George's Club of New York appeared at the TCC grounds (probably at Upper Canada College) ready to play a match at the invitation, previously received in New York, from a "Mr Phillpotts". There was a G.A. Phillpotts on the Toronto club roster at the time, a wicketkeeper of no mean talents, but he denied issuing any invitation. Friends confirmed he had been nowhere near New York on the day the "invitation" had been issued. The Americans were understandably annoyed; they had come more than 500 miles by private carriage, railway, stage coach, river boat, and lake schooner to be told they had not been invited. They retired from the field, grumping into their muttonchop whiskers, and registered in one of the city's hotels.

The gentlemen of Toronto were embarrassed; though the club was not to blame for the misunderstanding, still it was the name of the club that would suffer when the New Yorkers returned stateside. A committee of three, Colonel Mackenzie Fraser, W.H. Boulton, and John Barwick was appointed to meet with the Americans, offer a profound apology and make what offers it could to repair the damage of the practical joke.

The committee meeting with the Americans after they had refreshed themselves and dined, finally worked out a solution: The two teams were to play the following day, £50 per side, and the Torontonians to entertain the visitors at a dinner following.

On the appointed day the teams met; a complete account of the game was carried by the *New York Albion*:

At the conclusion of the match between the Toronto Cricket Club and the St George's Club of New York in 1840, the members of both teams were entertained at dinner with members of the Toronto Bowling Club invited to take part. The bowlers were officially represented by "John Ewart, Esquire, President of the Toronto Bowling Club," and a large turnout of members. At the time – 1840 – it is likely that the bowlers were already at play on the greens of the Caer Howell estate at the corner of University Avenue and College Street. It was to be two or three years before the cricketers moved in next door. The incident reveals, though, an informal but early and close relationship between the cricketers and bowlers.

The cricket match between the St. George's Club, of New York, and the Toronto Club, U.C., to which we alluded in a late *Albion*, came off at Toronto on Friday,... A large and highly respectable crowd was present to witness the progress of this truly noble and manly English sport, and the play went off with the greatest *éclât*. The most marked attention and civility was shown by the members of the Toronto Club, as well as by the inhabitants generally, to their friends of the New York club; and as both the clubs were composed entirely of Old Countrymen, it is hardly necessary to say that the harmony of feeling and warmth of welcome between the two amicably opposed parties was unqualified by any less grateful emotion. It is said and believed that the Toronto Club were not in their full strength, owing to the absence of some of their members from the city; but as we understand that it is purposed to play a return match in New York next spring, we hope to see their play in the full vigour, of their capabilities; when the Sons of St. George, here, will meet them again with pleasure and satisfaction, whatever may be the result.

The play commenced by the Toronto Club going in, with the Hon. Mr. Draper, Attorney-General, for their umpire. Mr. W. Howe acted as umpire for New York; and it is a pleasure to hear that no difficulties occurred, but that all their decisions were promptly obeyed.

The play was honoured by the presence of the Governor of the Province, Sir George Arthur, and part of his staff. The band, of the 34th Regiment were present, and played many beautiful and national airs during the match.

The following is the score of the play:-

TORONTO CLUB

First Innings		Second Innings	
Goring, c Wild	3	c Groom	3
Barber, b Gill	1	run out	16
Warren, b Gill	2	b Groom	0
Bliss (32nd. Regt.) run out	7	b Groom	9
Birch, run out	10	b Groom	6
Maddock, run out	9	b W. Russell	2
Winkworth, run out	1	c Stead	0
Marriott (32nd Regt.) not out	6	b Groom	7
Harrington, c Gill	0	c Green	1
Girdlestone, run out	4	not out	7
Spragge, c Wright	0	b Groom	1
			46
	43	Byes 6, wide balls 2	8
			54
Byes 6, wide balls 3	9		
	52	First innings	52
		Total	106

ST. GEORGE'S CLUB, NEW YORK

First Innings		Second Innings	
Gill, c Maddock	1	Wright, not out	3
W. Russell, c Barker	6	Wild, not out	5
Wright, b Winkworth	2		
H. Russell, b Winkworth	17	Wild ball	8
Tinson, b Winkworth	0		1
Wild, c Harrington	22		9
Weightman, b Winkworth	17		
Stead, b Winkworth	2	First innings	98
Wyvill, b Winkworth	0		
Green, not out	4	Total	107
	71		
Byes 13, wide balls 13,	26		
	98		

After the day's sport was concluded, the parties sat down to a splendid and sumptuous banquet, to which the St. George's had been invited by their hospitable Toronto opponents. Every delicacy of the season had been procured, the finest wines were drunk, loyal and social toasts prevailed, and good Old English hospitality, hearty welcome, and feelings of brotherhood were unequivocally manifested. The St. George's club have returned with emotions of the warmest respect for their brethren of Toronto, and with earnest desire to show their sense of hospitality and kindness they experienced by reciprocating it whensoever the the opportunity shall be offered.

The match caused some considerable excitement in and about Toronto, and there was an unanimous expression of admiration at the spirit of the St. George's Society, which could prompt them to travel so far for the promotion and encouragement of our glorious national game.

The *Albion's* arithmetic is atrocious, and the lineup shows but ten men playing for St George's. Still, correcting the scores—using the runs as shown—does not give a win to Toronto. It was a loss but the banquet which followed was consolation.

Of the banquet following the game, a meal at which W.H. Boulton the club president presided as toastmaster, a contemporary observer writes that the last toast, to the Sons of St George, St Patrick, St David and St Andrew was drunk "nine times nine," a feat of no mean proportions.

Despite the well intentioned plans, the game between Toronto and New York was not followed up. So far as can be determined no game was planned or played in 1841 or 1842. However, in 1843 the St George's team was again in Toronto, this time with a genuine invitation. A debate arose, though, when Toronto learned the New Yorkers had included three Philadelphia players on their squad. The Torontonians balked, refused to play.

Disaster—ill feelings, at the very least—was averted when the Guelph team agreed to meet with the visitors on the grounds of the Taddle. With the agreement of New York, Guelph added six players from Upper Canada College to strengthen its roster. The additional strength helped; Guelph scored 71 runs against the Americans' 33.

Toronto went south in September of the same year and beat St George's on its home ground by four wickets.

The play between the Toronto and Guelph clubs, and the New Yorkers generated an interest in a continuing series of matches. Negotiations by mail and some face-to-face meetings resulted in the first match of the US-Canada International Series. It was played on the mornings of 24 and 25 September 1844, at Manhattan, between elevens representing the United States and Canada. Ground rules adopted for the game specified that all hits would be run out, standard procedure for the day. Toronto took the match 145 to 122.

The Canadian roster was well laced with Toronto club members. George Barber was there, the only international match in which the master played. John Beverley Robinson Jr, now twenty-three years of age, was present in *his* only international appearance. Birch, who had played against New York in 1840, played in Manhattan, as did G.A. Phillpotts, in whose name the fake invitation sent St George's to Toronto. Other Toronto club players were Maddock, Freeling, Thompson, and French.

French was the Toronto Cricket Club professional. In the nineteenth century, however, the word professional meant a good deal more than it does today. French, it is true, instructed the members in the fine points of play and was enough of a diplomat to bowl easily until the members perfected their stance at the wicket. But in addition, French cared for the grounds and on occasion cooked for the members; his specialty was lamb chops in tomato sauce, said to be a delectable dish, enough to draw members from all sides of the city whether they chose to play cricket or not.

French's ministrations to the grounds were painstaking. The *Canadian Cricketer's Guide* of 1858 paid tribute to French's labours; of the Taddle grounds it said, "that 40 yards by 30 yards of velvety turf...forever rendered famous in the annals of cricket...cannot be surpassed in America."

In 1845, when the second match of the International Series was played, the locale was Montreal, presumably on the grounds that Montreal was more convenient, if not much closer, to New York than Toronto. At least three members of the TCC were represented on the Canadian team and the round trip to and from Montreal must have consumed the better part of a week. Most of the distance would have been covered by stage coach although the travellers may have broken the monotony of the trip with a day's jaunt by steamer. The match was played on the afternoon of 30 July 1845 and Canada won in two innings by 61 runs.

For the fortunes of the Toronto club, the middle years of the nineteenth century consolidated the gains made during the earlier years. The years saw, also, the emergence of another towering figure of Canadian cricket who impressed on the Toronto club, and the game in general, the force of his boundless enthusiasm and indomitable energy.

T. (for Thomas) D. Phillipps was the son of British parents, and his schoolteacher father early decided that his son's education in Canada was best entrusted to Upper Canada College. Young Phillipps soon immersed himself in the school's cricket program and, true to his character, almost immediately found himself on the organizing end.

In 1847, he wrote, he first took an active part in management "and it was as a nonconformist. For, conceiving that the boarding-house boys were monopolizing the grounds [at the college on King Street], implements, etc., of the cricket club to our almost entire exclusion, a number of us who were non-resident started a day-boys' club,...probably our best incentive was found in the permission of the committee of the Toronto club to practise daily on the outside of their crease...at that time the finest piece of turf used for that purpose in America."

But Phillipps was more than a pushy young schoolboy; that he was abundantly possessed of cricket talent would have been obvious to the Toronto club members from watching the youngster practise every day. In less than a year he had been selected for a place on a TCC eleven to play against the rifle brigade of the garrison. Phillipps was too modest to

Some thirty-odd years after it was built (this photograph was taken in 1869) Upper Canada College was showing signs of maturity; trees and vines had grown to help conceal the buildings' raw newness. The children in the foreground are not identified but may belong to various of the married masters' families.

reveal his own performance in this game but he provides this picture of H.J. Maddock, a senior member of the club who had played against New York in the game of 1844:

> That little man, H.J. Maddock, the first "slow" underhand bowler I ever saw, captured all of the opposing team, always famous for its batting, for a total of 16 runs, if I remember aright, clean bowled! By the way, he always wore a black beaver whether bowling or batting – the last of his race.

Not only was Phillipps invited to play for the Toronto club but the services of the club's professional, French, were provided for the UCC day boys without charge.

In 1852, while a theology student at Trinity College, Phillipps organized the college team.

Phillipps played with the Canadian eleven in the International Series of 1865 and fourteen years later, in 1879, was still a member of the team and selected to open the Canada batting. The only comment Phillipps is known to have made about his own play concerned a game he played in 1876 as an ex-student member of an UCC eleven.

> The last match in which I played as an ex-pupil of Upper Canada College was in 1876, when I had the good fortune to take the first ball and carry out my bat for 51, as many of our opponents scored in their two innings.

For most of his long and distinguished career the Reverend T.D. Phillipps played for the St Catharines Club. But he served the cause of cricket throughout Canada.

In September 1872 the Toronto club played host to a touring English team under Captain R.A. Fitzgerald which included the famous batsman, W.G. Grace. In a book about the tour, *Wickets in the West*, Fitzgerald reminisced about the Toronto hospitality.

> The Twelve were invited to a grand banquet given by members of the Royal Canadian Yacht Club. Their gallant Commodore, Dr. Hodder, presided. He was a venerable man, the White Admiral of the fleet. The club-house is on the shore of Lake Ontario. The evening was cheerful–speeches prolific–the Commodore very happy in his remarks–the Captain [the author, that is] in voice, repeating all the good things he had uttered elsewhere; but warming at the sight of the neat naval uniform worn by the members of the Club, expressed his conviction that so long as the Royal Canadian Yacht Club nurtured a gallant race of sailors, Canada need not fear for her inland waters.... There were other parties in the course of the week: private entertainments given by the worthy President, Mr. Heward and Mr. Patteson, celebrated for no speeches; rather disappointing to the Captain, who had prepared an original one.

As the nineteenth century glided towards its conclusion, another cricketing celebrity, from the Toronto club, came to prominence. Dyce W. Saunders first played cricket for his hometown team of Guelph and at the age of nineteen took part in his first international match with the US in 1881. It was the first of two dozen appearances in the International Series by the redoubtable Saunders.

Saunders's accomplishments are legendary; he was a wicketkeeper of extraordinary talents. In 1885, while still playing with Guelph, he had been co-opted to the All-Ontario team playing a touring English Gentlemen's eleven. On 10 and 11 September, on a pitch sodden by rain, the Ontario cricketers were drubbed unmercifully by the English tourists; in an account of the match written much later by one of the British players, Saunders is the only Canadian player to draw any praise: "Saunders kept wicket exceedingly well."

John Marder sums up Saunders's career in these words:

> He was educated at Trinity College, Port Hope, and was captain of cricket in 1879. He was a strong batsman with an upright style and was an excellent wicket-keeper. He played with Guelph and Toronto and toured England with the Canadian team of 1887. On that tour he scored 613 runs with an average of 23.58, being second in batting. His highest score was seventy-one against Gentlemen of Surrey at the Oval. He played in the International for twenty-four years, his last match taking place in 1905. In 1906 Dyce played a classic innings of 109 for Toronto v Philadelphia Pilgrims and again toured England with Toronto in 1922 [with Norman Seagram's team] when he was sixty years old.... Dyce was later termed the 'Grand Old Man' of Canadian cricket and died at London, Ontario, on 12 June 1930.

It is said that his is the only portrait of a Canadian cricket player to decorate the walls at Lord's.

DYCE W. SAUNDERS

* * *

The 1887 tour of England by the
Gentlemen of Canada produced many
results, not the least of which was a
book about the tour written by two
cricket club members of the team,
G.G.S. Lindsey, and Dyce Saunders.
Lindsey is shown standing, *extreme left,*
and Saunders is seated, *second from right.*
The young woman in this photograph,
and in the picture on page 50, is Mrs.
E.R. Ogden. Her husband, the team's
captain, is to the right of her in this
picture.

DINNER
TO
MR. NORMAN SEAGRAM'S
CANADIAN CRICKET TEAM
AT
THE HOUSE OF COMMONS,
Monday, July 31st, 1922.

◇

By Invitation of
SIR ROWLAND BLADES, Bart., M.P.

For fifty years, more or less, the Taddle had been home to the Toronto Cricket Club. For all this time the ownership of the property remained with the Boulton family, which was always pleased to play host to the club, often enough contributing members to the executive, or the team, or both.

In the mid-nineties, however, the growth of the city, straining north, put the inevitable squeeze on the Taddle. The grounds which had become known to scores of North American and European cricketers were too valuable as real estate to remain "vacant". The property was subdivided and the club was homeless.

(To the east of the Taddle, the old Caer Howell Hotel continued in business for a few years, gaining in patronage from the university more than enough customers to make up for the departed cricketers. Later again—in 1910—what had been an elegant spa for the fashionable set of early York and Toronto became a common tavern hangout for toughs of the city's "Ward" and its licence was finally revoked.)

The Toronto Cricket Club became a vagabond of sports. It made arrangements with the university to play on the lawn in front of University College and, in the middle nineties, played and practised for a couple of years on vacant ground at the corner of Bloor Street and Devonshire Place, a location now occupied by Varsity Stadium.

In 1906 the club moved, at the invitation of Trinity College Cricket Club, to the "Back Campus," that considerable stretch of grass that extends north from University College to Hoskin Avenue. In return for the use of the Trinity College locker rooms, the Toronto club extended to all Trinity cricketers courtesy membership in the club.

In 1926, after thirty-some years of playing on fields belonging to other clubs, the TCC made its final move to the present grounds in Armour Heights. Several members formed the Cricket Development Limited to purchase about thirteen acres of property fronting on Wilson Avenue. Through a series of legal documents, certain parts of the property were deeded to the TCC and the rest leased. One of the principals in Cricket Development Limited was Norman Seagram, surely one of the most dedicated cricketers produced to that time.

Seagram was a member of the Waterloo, Ontario, family of distillers and horseracers, a stockbroker, a man of means. Earlier, in the first years of the 1920s, he conceived the idea that an English tour would be advantageous for a representative Canadian team; the competition would be stiff and consistent and a Canadian team would benefit.

Seagram was not speculating idly. In 1910 he had been a member of the Canadian Zingari team during its English tour. He knew the value of British competition.

By 1922 he had put his team together—S.R. Harper, A.E. Mix, C.R. Somerville, H.J. Lounsborough, H. Dean (manager), G.E.D. Greene, A.M. Inglis, H.S. Reid, R.D. Hague, Dyce W. Saunders, P.E. Henderson, H.W. Wookey, S.R. Saunders, T.W. Seagram, V.R. Mustard, and L.M. Rathbun. In eleven matches the Canadians drew seven and lost four. Everywhere they played they were praised for their play and their sportsmanship; among other social events they were tendered a dinner at the House of Commons by Sir Rowland Blades, MP.

University College looms in the background as Taddle Creek meanders past
on its way to the lake. The creek gave
its name to the cricket club's pitch.

On his return home from the English tour, Seagram plunged into organization of the Cricket Development Limited and in 1926 (and for some years after), when the club opened on Wilson Avenue, he served as captain.

For all his wealth and qualities of leadership, Seagram was a modest man. It never struck him as unusual that during the first, uncertain years at the new location, when the club's finances were rather more than usually straitened, it should be he, Norman Seagram, who personally held the deeds to building lots that had previously belonged to Cricket Development Limited. In the most literal sense, Seagram was, more than once, the saviour of the Toronto Cricket Club.

The club built a clubhouse, a gracious, multi-gabled structure, reminiscent of an English country home. As already mentioned, a fire in 1952 partially destroyed the building but it was rebuilt; fire insurance, however, could never replace the invaluable cricket archives lost in the fire.

With the amalgamation in 1956-7 of the cricket, curling, and skating clubs, new premises were required. The former building was moved to the eastern end of the grounds (more or less where the parking lot is located at present) and continued to serve as a clubhouse for the year while the new clubhouse was built. It was then demolished and the entire property became the Toronto Cricket, Skating, and Curling Club as we know it today.

*   *   *

It is entirely fitting that, on the eve of the TCSCC's 150th anniversary, the cricket team set forth from the present clubhouse in September 1976 to compete for the J. Ross Robertson Challenge Trophy, emblematic of Canadian cricket sovereignty. On 4 and 5 September the TCSCC eleven won the trophy in a match with the Victoria Alcos Cricket Club at Beaconhill Park on Vancouver Island. The Toronto team, captained by Tony Clarke, consisted of Charles De Souza, Peter Burn, Chris Chappell, Pat Pisani, John Harvey, Moshin Keshavji, Alister Hays, Norm Bracht, Debbie Aldridge (scorer), Ric Stevens, Les Pereira, Ron Aldridge, Upender Sood, and Keith Gouevia.

The *Flash* of Youth!

Competition skating is a sport for young legs, shapely if possible but muscular of necessity. Champions peak early, hold their titles for a year, maybe two, and then yield to the demands of still younger legs and insistent ambitions. From the earliest years the skating club stressed the fun of skating and only gradually did the rigours of competition skating become part of the club's regimen. Here is an album of some of the young faces – and their young, muscular legs – that have brought honour and renown to the club over the decades.

PREVIOUS PAGE, TOP
A quartet of Montgomery "Bud" Wilson, Maud and Cecil Smith, and Jack Eastwood won the Canadian fours competition for three years running starting in 1925.

BOTTOM
Eastwood and Maud Smith competed in the junior pairs competition as well without taking honours.

Frances Dafoe and Norris Bowden (above) brought consistent honours to the skating club throughout the early and middle years of the 1950s. For four years starting in 1952 they were Canadian pairs champions. Between 1953 and 1955 they ruled as North American champs, and for 1954 and 1955 they held the world title as well.

Barbara Wagner and Robert Paul (opposite) made a modest beginning by capturing the Canadian junior pairs in 1954 at Calgary as shown here. Taking 1955 as a sabbatical year, they sprang back in 1956 winning the Canadian senior pairs, a title they almost totally usurped. They held it, without break, through the 1960 competition and won the Olympic title the same year.

Two bright lights that flashed into brilliance in the 1950s were Hayes Alan Jenkins *(left)*, and Roberta Laurance *(right)*. Jenkins owned the senior men's titles in the US, North America, and the world for the three years from 1953 to 1955.

Miss Laurance was a stylish and piquant competitor in the latter years of the decade. She is shown here accepting the plaudits of the spectators at the conclu-sion of her free skating performance in 1958.

Recipe for a skating star: Take one pair of healthy, youthful legs; take one burning ambition; mix well with time. Time . . . it's the secret ingredient of a skater's success. Time . . . mind-numbing hours spent in endless repetition of the same figure. Time . . . seconds, minutes, hours that add up to days and even months of every year spent on perfecting one's smallest movement. In performance not a flaw will show, no effort will seem to have been expended. It looks so easy – graceful and easy. The casual smiles of the youngsters mask a herculean effort and an almost frightening investment of time.

The recipe is almost infallible provided time enough is available.

  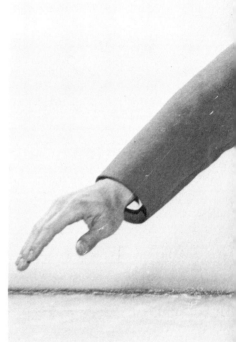

Wendy Griner *(above)*, Leslie Black *(right)*, and Donald Jackson *(opposite)* are typical of the champions produced by the club, champions who have been competitors of world standing by means of large dashes of native talent and the expenditure of hour after incredible hour of exhausting, endless, debilitating practice.

Generally considered to be one of the most exciting male skaters to appear in international competitions, Toller Cranston *(overleaf)* is a flamboyant star who has forced the crusty crew of judges to be much more tolerant in its marking of free skating exercises.

ABOVE, LEFT

In 1965 the pair of Linda Trasker and Allan Carson display their synchronized form in the final competition of the season.

ABOVE

Barbara Berezowski and David Porter glide into the finale of their senior dance routine which won for them the country's top honours in 1976.

Petra Burka *(opposite)* ruled supreme as the Canadian, North American, and world senior lady's champion in the middle 1960s. In addition, she won the Lou Marsh and other awards.

CHAPTER FOUR

Skating:
An Age-old Sport
Revived

Skating was the sport practised earliest in Canada and, apart from newly invented games such as basketball, one of the latest to get organized into clubs.

In 1604, Pierre du Gua, the Sieur de Monts, landed a small force of settlers on an island in the Bay of Fundy. Included in the party as a navigator was the young Samuel de Champlain who in a few years' time was to leave his mark on the new land. De Monts's men built a rough and temporary village and by the time winter descended, the first permanent European settlement of Canada had been well established. During the winter months the men amused themselves with hunting and "skating on the ponds." But it is not until the middle of the nineteenth century that skating clubs became common.

What happened? What prevented Canadian skaters from banding together in clubs for the promotion of their favourite sport? The answer is at once simple and complex. The problem was competitiveness – or, rather, the *lack* of competitiveness.

Skating was seen mainly as a means of locomotion; trappers, hunters, outdoorsmen, used skates as a means of getting around faster on a trapline or a hunting range. Skating was, in frankest terms, a money-making means of propulsion, a necessity, not a recreation.

Even when the recreational aspects of skating were realized it was as speed skating that the sport surfaced. In 1854, we read, three officers in the Montreal barracks raced each other from that city to Quebec on the frozen St Lawrence. But it was years before the graceful, balletic style, originally known as "fancy" skating was to become popular.

When skating did become a leisure-time activity it was indulged as a healthy, convivial entertainment rather than a competitive sport. Outdoor ice made uneven by repeated thaws and freezing weather, might be unacceptable for curlers, but proved little hindrance to the enjoyment of pleasure skaters. Curlers solved their problems by building sheds to protect the ice from sun and snow. It would be some years before the requirements of competitiveness forced the skaters to abandon their outdoor rinks for the more reliable surface of covered ice.

It was the 1860s before Jackson Haines, the American ballet master, conceived the idea of marrying the movements of classical ballet to the swooping grace of skating. Haines toured Quebec and Ontario giving demonstrations of his new "figures"; when he went to Europe in the late 1870s he was followed by young Louis Rubenstein of Montreal. Rubenstein learned well from the master; within a few years Louis was the acknowledged champion of Canada although no competition was held to decide the winner. In 1885 and 1889 he won the US amateur championships.

In 1890 Rubenstein represented Canada in the first (although unofficial) world championship held at St Petersburg, Russia. He placed first. His performance was dazzling; it was said he could cut a figure and retrace it three or four times without blurring the original outline. He returned home a hero and with his remarkable feat, catapulted figure skating into the Canadian consciousness. Given the impetus of Rubenstein's achievement it was only a few years before Canadian skaters were ap-

Pleasure skating in Canada extends back further than do written records but it was only in the latter years of the nineteenth century that clubs were organized. The watercolour sketch by architect John Howard was made in 1835 and, in addition to being an animated scene of skaters at play, shows sleighing, ice boating and ice cutting as well. Howard had trained as a surveyor and his scenes of everyday life are valuable records of the streetscape as well. The three large buildings labelled "2" are the government buildings shown also on page 71. The several buildings numbered "8" are remnants of the earliest Fort York.

pearing regularly in the top ranks of the world's best.

The year following Rubenstein's triumph in Russia, George Meagher, also of Montreal, went all the way to another (unofficial) world championship. His *Lessons in Skating*, published in 1900, clinched the popularity of the sport. Skating clubs were founded and indoor rinks proliferated. The Canadian Amateur Skating Association was formed in 1886, the figure skating department in 1913. In the latter year there were but eight member clubs; today the number has grown to almost one thousand.

Just as cricket had been played in York before the Toronto Cricket Club was formed, (and, as we shall see, just as curling had been played long before the Toronto Curling Club became a reality), so had Toronto's skaters been skimming around Toronto Bay long before anyone thought to pin a club label on them. John G. Howard, the architect of Upper Canada College, had painted skating scenes in the early 1830s (see above). Throughout the middle years of the century Toronto newspapers occasionally carried accounts of festival-like congregations of skaters on the bay, the frozen surface of the Don, and even on sloughs and swamps within the city itself. Taddle Creek, the meandering brook that gave its name to the cricket club's first home, formed a moderate-sized pond on the grounds of what is now the campus of the University of Toronto. Standing about where Hart House is located, the pond was a favourite skating place as soon as it had frozen over.

In the years before the skating club was formed, the Victoria Club, the corporate identity of the Toronto Curling Club, rented its various ice surfaces to non-member skaters. (Indeed, for a number of years, the parent curling club was known as the Victoria Skating and Curling Association.)

There is a strong suspicion that an organization of Toronto skaters – call it a club, fraternal organization, no matter – existed long before one bearing the name Toronto Skating Club came into existence. Hanging in the clubhouse of the TCSCC today is a medal awarded in 1865 to Lewellyn H. Robertson by the "Toronto Skating Club". The date is thirty years before the official founding of the club.

In the next chapter of this book is detailed the events which took place in early 1877 when the Governor General, Lord Dufferin, and Lady Dufferin opened the Toronto Curling Club's premises on Adelaide Street West. As a memento of the occasion, Lady Dufferin received a pair of presentation skates from the "skating department" of the club.

It seems reasonable to suggest that the "skating department" was a club within a club, a skating wing of the Toronto Curling Club. (The name, Victoria Skating and Curling Association, bears out this assumption.) If this guess comes close to the truth, the amalgamation of curling and skating clubs in 1957 was more of a reunion than an introduction.

Speculation aside, the Skating Club of Toronto was formed in 1895, goaded into existence largely by the efforts of May Dawson and her sis-

A precursor of the skating club's carnival is shown in this *Canadian Illustrated News* drawing from 1896. Although rendered in black and white, the scene fairly bursts with colour as skaters in costumes that are gay, romantic, fantastic, and imaginative swoop and whirl about the ice.

ter, Mrs Carrington Smith. Miss Dawson had been converted to figure skating in her native Montreal, probably in the wake of publicity attendant upon the activities of Louis Rubenstein and George Meagher. When she moved to Toronto she was disappointed to find no clubs organized to promote her favourite sport; she enlisted her sister's support, signed on other enthusiasts, and declared the club a going concern.

It wasn't — not quite.

It seems not to have held any business meetings. Or it didn't keep minutes. Or the minutes have been lost. At any rate, we know very little about the earliest years of the club. We can get occasional glimpses from newspaper reports.

The club held its first skating meet in early December and the *Globe* reported:

> The first skate of the season, so far as the new Club at the Victoria rink is concerned, came off most successfully on Monday night when the ice in that popular rink was covered with a goodly representation of the youth, beauty, and fashion of Toronto. The inauguration of this Club is due to Col. Sweny and Mrs. Sweny of Rohallion, while for the successful carrying out of the plans proposed and indeed the greater part of the hard work incidental to the beginning of any organization, much credit is to be given to Mr. Rex Macdonald, the Secretary of the Club.
>
> While most of the ladies and gentlemen on the ice Monday night were good skaters — some indeed being wonderfully expert and graceful — still there were others who are as yet novices in the art, but their enthusiasm will doubltless soon enable them to overcome all difficulties. To the time of excellent music a very pretty set of Lancers was danced and also waltzes were enjoyed, the Misses Dawson in particular waltzing most gracefully. Mrs. Sweny is another who looks particularly graceful as she flits about.

Tradition holds that the club held a "carnival" in its first year and there is little reason to doubt it. From the earliest years in York, one of the most popular pastimes had been grand balls for which men and women concocted the most fanciful and outrageous costumes imaginable. When indoor skating became popular these mammoth masquerades took to the ice as precursors of the carnivals the club was to stage later. In the *Mail and Empire* of 2 December 1896 a columnist reported that "the members of the Skating Club will be on the ice Thursday afternoon at the Victoria Rink. The season promises to be one of great enthusiasm. The most fascinating costumes are only awaiting the opening event to see the light of day."

By 1898 the club was undergoing some kind of a reorganization. The following notice was mailed to all club members in November.

18 AND 20 KING ST. WEST
TORONTO

It is proposed to secure the exclusive use of a skating rink for an evening and an afternoon in each week during the skating season.

It is suggested that the number of skaters be limited to 150 at $4.00 each, which will raise a sum sufficient to defray the expense for ice and music.

The limited number, it is thought, will prevent any overcrowding.

If you wish to join in this arrangement, will you kindly notify Mr. Geo. C. Heward, 18 and 20 King Street West, Toronto, on or before the 1st December next?

If no reply is received from you by that date, it will be presumed that you do not wish to subscribe, and the vacancy caused by your refusal will be otherwise filled.

LT. COL. OTTER
ARCH'D H. CAMPBELL
W.A.H. KERR
J.P. HODGINS
J.H. MOSS
G.C. HEWARD

November 24, 1898.

That some kind of shaking up had taken place is confirmed by a report in the *Globe* of 12 December 1898:

The Skating Club that for some years past held its meetings at the Victoria rink having disbanded at the close of last winter, some of the more enthusiastic members have this year arranged to meet at the Mutual Street rink. The exclusive use of this rink has been obtained for Monday evening, 8 to 10:30 o'clock and Thursday afternoon, 4 to 6:30 o'clock. In addition to this, Club members showing badges will be permitted to use the rink at other times when it is not open to the public and not engaged for hockey. The membership has been limited to 150 and it is expected that keen skaters will be able to dance, cut figures or skate straight-away on really good ice without repetition of any of the discomfort that may have arisen in past years from overcrowding. The first skating will probably be on Monday, December 19. Mr. George C. Heward, of 18 and 20 King Street West is Club Secretary.

At the end of the 1898-9 season, the *Mail and Empire* said, "To a few congenial spirits who love skating for sport's sake the meetings of the Skating Club at the Mutual Street rink have no doubt been delightful." But something was missing. The paper added, "But to the outsider, even on the guest night, there is a lack of 'go' that makes itself felt."

Something of the "lack of go" must have communicated itself to the members as well as to the press. A general meeting was called for the evening of 21 November 1899 and the Skating Club of Toronto was reorganized, top to bottom.

The name was changed to the Toronto Skating Club, a constitution was adopted and minutes of meetings were to be taken, a board of management was elected to supervise the club's activities. George C. Heward

was elected as chairman. Finally, the meeting decided that the members should return to the Victoria Rink, that membership should be limited to 250 persons, and that annual dues were to be four dollars. Members of recent ice or house committees will be interested to learn that to rent the Victoria Rink for every Monday evening and Thursday afternoon during the whole season cost but $325.

For the first few years the fortunes of the club were uneven. Membership first increased, then declined. Skating was shifted from the Victoria Rink to Mutual Street to the Caledonia Skating and Curling Association. Then back to the Victoria Rink. Some years there were small surpluses in the club's operating budget; most years there were small deficits; in almost every year it was the club's carnival that made the difference between the red and black sides of the ledger.

In 1900 the annual meeting adopted a resolution asking that the club sponsor "if possible, an extra afternoon per week, without

Although the Toronto Skating Club was founded in 1895, a considerable body of evidence exists to show that the club was in operation much earlier. This drawing, from 1836, shows a group receiving some kind of instruction before starting a skating session. The rink was located on the scene of the present Allen Garden (early buildings are shown *left background*) and Sherbourne Street runs north to the horizon, *right.*

band, . . . for the purpose of encouraging figure skating for which so few facilities have been offered in the past." The extra work was worth it, because the following year the annual report claimed there had been a marked improvement in members' skating, figure skating in particular.

The years passed slowly, pleasantly; decisions were made and steps were taken that can be seen to be historic only when filtered through the lens of time.

In February of 1908 the club's first intramural competitions began; Mrs Bingham Allan won the women's competition, A.R. Martin the men's. A few days later John J. Cawthra won the second place in the Minto Skating Club's annual competitions; it is the first reference to interclub participation by TSC members.

In 1911 Arthur Ernest Kirkpatrick first took on the responsibilities of TSC chairman; it was the beginning of a long and progressive relationship. In 1912 the club hired its first professional, George Thomson.

During the first world war the Toronto Skating Club hibernated; it remained very much alive as an organization but was quiescent, nonactive. In December of 1918 the club met again under the chairmanship of (by this time) Lieutenant-Colonel A.E. Kirkpatrick. The club refused with thanks the offer of the Amateur Skating Association to donate a cup for the encouragement of figure skating within the membership. The reason: The club lacked the facilities necessary to provide potential competitors with sufficient practice time. The decision was the first move, albeit a negative one, in a concerted effort to provide the club members with more readily available ice.

For some time various pressures had been forcing the club towards its own clubhouse. On the one hand, the growing popularity of skating in general, and figure skating in particular, forced the club to bargain for more and more ice time. In some years the club used several different rinks, some indoor and some outdoor hockey cushions. It was a tendency which split the membership, literally.

On the other hand, ice time was becoming more and more expensive, as were most other services and goods. The resultant squeeze is best summed up in the words of an unpublished history of the club:

> For nearly a quarter of a century the members had led a nomadic life looking for available if not suitable ice. In different seasons they skated at the Victoria rink, Caledonia rink, Mutual Street rink, Granite rink (on Church Street), Varsity Stadium, Aura Lee and Ravina rinks. Generally there were only a few sessions, often at inconvenient hours . . . . the rentals absorbed a large part of the revenues. It is true that the members' fees were low but they were quite enough for the accommodation obtained . . . . As the Club grew rink rentals rose rapidly. The climax was reached when the Arena Gardens asked $3,500 for the privilege of skating one evening and two afternoons . . .

For some years the membership had been fond of discussing the "just-suppose" proposition: "Just suppose we had our *own* rink . . . ." The grandeur or paucity of the dream depended on the imagination of the dreamer. Few had the audacity to speculate on *artificial* ice for the club's exclusive use but that was the decision of the 1921 annual meeting.

A property had been purchased—568 Dupont Street, an address which was to become indelibly etched on the minds of members—and a separate limited company incorporated, the Toronto Winter Club Limited, to hold and administer it.

The location was well chosen; next door to the site was the plant of a company manufacturing ice cream. During the winter season—precisely the time of the year the club required ice—the plant's production of super-cooled brine was not required for making ice cream. It was an ideal arrangement for the club and the makers of ice cream. A five-year agreement was signed and the Toronto Skating Club became the world's first with its own artificial ice rink. (Later, the club installed its own ice maker.)

For thirty-six years "568" remained home for the Toronto Skating Club. The building was enlarged, changed, renovated, and altered but throughout its existence as the TSC headquarters it became the recognized world centre of expertise in staging ice spectaculars. It was with the achievement of the building at 568 Dupont Street that the TSC's reputation as world champions in the production of ice carnivals was set and consolidated.

The carnival.

The TSC's carnival was often said to be "ballet on ice", a not unreasonable claim when it is remembered that Jackson Haines, the first man to commit figures to paper, was primarily a ballet master. Sometimes the carnival went further and borrowed directly from classical ballet as in this example in which Jack Eastwood and Veronica Clarke skate the leads in *Swan Lake.*

What can be said that has not already been said? What words can possibly convey the sense of magic that pervaded the yearly spectacle? Before attempting to describe what the carnival was, it would be helpful to say what it was *not*.

Most importantly, perhaps, the carnival was not a local phenomenon. Certainly, the majority of its performers and production personnel were members of the Toronto Skating Club and, in that sense, were local talent. But as a spectacle, as a predictably excellent demonstration of show business polish, it was an international event.

In the heyday of the carnival, ticket orders poured in from the United States in numbers that still boggle the imagination. Delegations from Cleveland, Buffalo, Pittsburgh, New York City, Chicago, hired buses and train coaches to transport them to Toronto. Enthusiasts from as far as Moncton and St Louis journeyed every year to watch the show. One year the club's directors counted postmarks on letters requesting tickets; 249 different centres other than Toronto were represented. Most years, even when the carnival ran for five nights in the huge Maple Leaf Gardens, the entire allocation of seats was sold in the first twenty-four hours of sale.

Second, the carnival was not a professional ice show, in the sense that performers and backstage personnel were paid. (That the carnival gave rise to professional ice shows, though, we shall later see.) The club often hired professional skaters to round out a program. Skating comedians, for example, were often hired to provide notes of levity between spectacles. By and large, however, the talent was not paid. (Considering that the carnival often had casts of several hundred, it is unlikely that the proportion of professional talent ever exceeded one percent of the total.) The skaters were dedicated amateurs, all members all of the TSC. Neither the carnivals themselves, nor the uncounted hours of rehearsal time, were paid for.

Finally, the carnivals were not amateurish; that is, they were not inept, depending more on a sympathetic audience of family and friends than on an achievement of professional values. Produced and performed by amateurs, admittedly, but to professional standards of the highest kind.

As has been said, the carnivals began as a kind of mass masquerade party on ice; participants dressed in fanciful or outlandish costumes, paraded about the rink and socialized over the tea table. What set the TSC carnival apart from those of other clubs was the decision in 1919 to impose a theme. Costumes were no longer left to the individual's ingenuity, but designed and made as part of a larger pattern that encompassed the carnival as a whole. It was a step that led to successively greater accomplishments.

There was a kind of chest-bursting pride associated with the TSC carnivals. For participants, of course, the privilege of taking part was vastly appreciated. But for Torontonians in general, even for those who had never slipped a foot into a skate boot, the carnival was a source of civic pride. The club recognized that its production was a civic landmark and paid tribute in its 1938 program to the support it had received: The carnival, it said:

is in reality a great community enterprise. Its successful development has resulted from a kind of informal partnership between the Toronto Skating Club, who provided management and skaters, and the citizens of Toronto, who furnished support, encouragement, constructive criticism and co-operative assistance of every kind.

In everything associated with ice carnivals – costumes, music, lighting, properties, special effects – the Toronto Club was the innovator. One present member of the TCSCC remembers when the carnival managers used fluorescent costumes and "black" light for the first time:

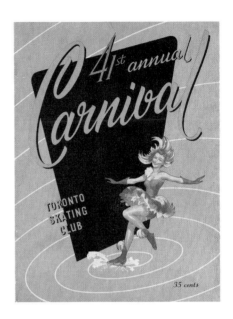

> The effect was spectacular. With the normal house lights out and the "black" lights on, the costumes glowed with brilliant luminescence. In addition, we'd painted the ice with large circles of fluorescent paint; the disembodied bodies of the skaters seemed to glide – to float, almost – from circle to circle. Just a splendid effect.
>
> Well, some members of a Cleveland club were in the audience and they later contacted us about finding out how the effect was achieved. Naturally, we told them – we were always happy to share our techniques with other clubs. We showed them how to get the special effect on the costumes, where to get the "black" light, how to paint the bullseyes on the ice.
>
> Next year we were invited to send a group from Toronto to see the club's first effort at producing a carnival. When it came time for the "black" light number, the first skater stepped on to the ice, the house lights went down, the "black" light came up, and the audience almost brought the roof down with applause. Very pretty. The skater started out, made the first jump to a painted circle – and disaster! You couldn't see exactly what happened but obviously she had fallen. From the antics of her fluorescent costume you could tell she was picking herself up and going on. She spun about for a few seconds and then tried the jump to the next circle. Bingo, she's down again. After that the skaters avoided the circles and everything went okay.
>
> After the show was over we found out they had painted the circles *right on the ice surface* without covering them with another thin layer of ice.

The Toronto newspapers deserve a fair degree of credit in publicizing the carnival. Their reviews were unfailingly enthusiastic, sometimes almost embarrassingly fulsome. Augustus Bridle, the venerable culture critic of the Toronto *Star*, almost babbled in his 1942 review: "This year's carnival exceeds even technicolor movies in revels of beauty in colour. It makes even the fabulous Ballet Theatre, here a month ago, seem trivial in comparison.... brilliant with scintillating colour...long lines of super-ballet motion like a magnificat of some old quadrille.... Some years ago I first compared the carnival to a great ballet."

As far back as 1922 the *Telegram* was good naturedly complaining, "The pity of it is that the huge arena [Arena Gardens], packed to the roof, could not begin to satisfy the crowds that wanted seats. It could not even fill the demands of friends of the Skating Club and the general public lost a spectacle that, for sheer beauty, has seldom been equalled in

Frances Dafoe Melnick was a superb skater and doubled for many years as the carnival's costume designer.

Fran Claudet, a graduate of the club's training program, was for twenty years choreographer with the Ice Follies.

this city. To see it was to be a better Canadian. For what could you not hope from a land that had a national sport that was so beautiful a thing."

From the earliest days, some of the carnival's most popular numbers were those featuring the junior members of the club. Their popularity was not always for the precision and competence of the youngsters – although they trained like troopers to become letter perfect. As often as not the appeal was the determined work of one or two children who were simply too small to keep in step. Everybody is a real or potential parent; every parental heart warmed to watch children.

Sometimes, the carnival committee was urged to shift a program about to put the juniors' numbers closer to the end of the show. It was often a tempting request; every director wants to conclude his show to tempestuous applause. Throughout the carnival's history, however, the needs of the youngsters were kept to the forefront. In later years brigades of taxis were organized to be waiting at the rink at appointed hours; as the children finished their last number, they changed and were whisked home in speed and safety. The adults relaxed their control on the last night when the young performers were allowed to watch the whole carnival from beginning to end.

Some years the club's own orchestra was supplemented with other musical groups, on occasion the Toronto Symphony Orchestra under Ernest (later Sir Ernest) MacMillan, at other times the military bands of various regiments. As in every other aspect of carnival production, the musical scoring blazed trails that other carnivals and ice shows were to follow from that day to this.

We have spoken of the carnival's impact as a cultural achievement on the city and its citizens, but there was another aspect of its success that is often forgotten. During the years of the second world war the bulk of the carnival profits went to the Canadian Red Cross. More than fifty thousand dollars – much more – were poured into Red Cross activities, much of the money supplying the capital needed to establish the Canadian branch's unique and famous free blood-transfusion service. It is a record of which the club members may be justly proud.

As many an institution before and since, the carnival had planted the seed of its own destruction. Its success was too obvious, too attractive not to draw competitors. In many respects the Toronto Skating Club almost encouraged competition by its open-handed sharing of techniques and procedures. But it would be foolish to suggest that the "secrets" should not have been shared. In the first place, the carnival was a public spectacle; few "secrets" remain secret when they are performed openly before thousands of spectators for three, four, and five nights in succession. Even more importantly, a refusal to share a knowledge gained in carnival production would have aborted the very purpose for which the carnival had been established.

Almost from the beginning – certainly from 1919 – the carnival's purpose had been clearly defined as a two-part objective: To encourage the promotion of figure skating as a sport, and second, to provide the TSC with sufficient funds to carry out an enlarged program of training.

Certainly the club's ability to train young skaters was of great importance. But it was not necessarily more important than the more general purpose of popularizing the sport. Both goals were important and both were stressed.

Four times in the late twenties and early thirties, the carnival directors had hired the professional ice comedians, Shipstad and Johnson. In 1934 the two men assembled and staged a large ice show in the Chicago Stadium, an event which was widely heralded as the birth of "a big show on ice". Again, in 1934 Sonja Henie, the world and Olympic title holder, performed with the TSC carnival and went on to form her own professional ice show incorporating many of the techniques and routines first developed by the Toronto amateurs.

At first, the touring shows presented minimal competition to the carnival which survived and, for a time, even seemed to thrive. But the competition for the customers' dollar was intense; publicity and paid advertising for the professional companies was heavy and insistent. Eventually the tide turned in their favour and the TSC carnival was quietly laid to rest.

The professional shows had a number of advantages over the TSC carnival. First, they carried a smaller roster of personnel, miniscule in comparison with the carnival's cast of characters. Second, the cost of production – immense in every case – was spread over a whole skating season instead of being limited to a two- to five-night stand. Third, the length of the professional season meant that the cost of rehearsal time, cost which must be recouped, was spread over a much longer performance schedule and was not as costly, per performance, as it was for the club.

At first there was a good deal of bitterness in the club that ideas, innovations, plans developed first for the encouragement of amateur skating should have been lifted from that context and translated into pure profit making. In time, however, the bitterness eased. If "imitation is the sincerest form of flattery," then the club has been complimented indeed.

Now there is little more than sadness. Sadness for the passing of a fine tradition that grew and flourished briefly.

Within the club, of course, the carnival's seminal role in the big modern ice show of today is recognized and accepted. Outside the club, however, there are generations coming to maturity who have never seen a skating club carnival and who know nothing of the club's part. It is part of the anniversary celebrations to burnish the legends – as much as the hardware – and display them in their full glory.

The carnival as a mammoth, money-making, civic enterprise was finished. But the spirit remains in the more modest club carnival staged every third year on the TCSCC's own ice. Over three evenings and two matinee performances, young club skaters (primarily in the five- to fifteen-year-old age group) get a chance to show their skills before family and friends. It is an important part of their training, especially if their eyes are set on competition.

An additional aspect of the carnival survives in the club's annual participation in the Christmas tree lighting ceremony which takes place annually at Nathan Phillips's Square in downtown Toronto.

True to its mandate to teach, train, and produce better skaters, the Toronto Skating Club throughout the years of the carnival's ascendancy,

The success story of Barbara Wagner and Robert Paul is unmatched in the annals of pairs skating. Their story is best summed up by Nancy and Maxwell Howell in *Sports and Games in Canadian Life*: "In 1956 the names of Barbara Wagner and Robert Paul were not well known . . . . The following year their names soared to the top . . . [They] won both the Canadian Junior and Senior pairs title, the North American title at Colorado Springs, and the world title . . . . At the 1960 Winter Olympics at Squaw Valley, [they] won gold medals for their exquisite performances in the pairs . . . A few days later, at the World Championships held in Vancouver, British Columbia, their names once more topped the list of winners. Their skating skill and achievements were such that they will always be counted among Canada's most adept, graceful, and successful figure skaters."

In 1962 at Prague, Don Jackson electrified the judges with the first publicly performed triple lutz, a feat which won him the world title with a perfect score. His accomplishment in world competition was unmatched until 1974 but by that time, in 1973, another TCSCC member, Vernon Taylor, had performed the jump in a national competition.

turned out an increasingly productive flow of superior skaters. Through the twenties and thirties the club hired the best professionals it could find, and worked diligently to promote high standards in judging.

The strength of the skating section has never been considered to be in the champions but in the total membership. However, some of the skaters achieved world renown through the work of dedicated professionals and talented, hard-working skaters.

It is noted that the club's strength built slowly. The records of the Canadian Figure Skating Championships are complete since 1905 but it was not until 1924 that a Toronto Skating Club member, Constance Wilson, won a Canadian championship. Since that date there have been very few years when the Toronto Skating Club did not place champions on the list if not, indeed, dominate all competitions.

Many members have worked long hours and with great intensity but have stayed behind the scenes, out of the limelight, and to these people must go great credit. Colonel Clifford Sifton, Norman Samuel, Donald Cruickshank, Jack Eastwood, and Ralph McCreath must be recognized, as must Donald Gilchrist.

Montgomery "Bud" Wilson won world-wide fame skating both in the men's seniors and in the pairs, skating with his sister, Constance. Bud Wilson first won the senior men's Canadian championship in 1929 and his name was noted throughout most of the next decade in world skating circles.

Osborne Coulson first attracted attention by winning the senior men's Canadian championship in 1936. Veronica Clarke and Ralph McCreath were winners of both Canadian and North American championships. Barbara Wagner and Robert Paul brought glory to themselves and to the club through winning the Canadian, North American, World, and Olympic championships.

Barbara Ann Scott occasionally trained at the club and brought with her a great deal of fame although she never did skate as a member of the club. Suzanne Morrow and Wallace Distelmeyer won Canadian and North American championships.

Toller Cranston was generally acknowledged to be the most exciting free skater in the world in 1976 but was only able to achieve a bronze in the men's singles in Innsbruck, Austria.

Throughout its history the club's professionals have been in the lead in producing champions for whom the club has become famous. All professionals contributed their share but special mention must be made of Sheldon Galbraith, Ellen Burka, Bruce Hyland, and Osborne Coulson.

Space does not permit the mention of all the champions. Starting from a humble beginning, the club has grown to produce some of the best skaters in the world.

On 24 February 1966 at Varsity Stadium in Toronto, fifteen-year-old Petra Burka became the first woman in history to successfully complete, in competition, the triple salchow.

CARNIVAL

In 1962 the club staged its first
abbreviated carnival in the new
clubhouse. In a presentation of
"Maria," Paulette Doan *(third from
left* in hat and party dress)
played the heroine while J.F. "Dinty"
Moore was the puppet master.
Later, Miss Doan with Ken Ormsby
were North American and Canadian
champions in the dance.

Scenes from the 1973 bursary dinner:

Top, three of the winners – Toller Cranston, Karen Magnussen, and Donald Knight – ...t on from amateur honours to professional ice shows. *Middle,* a tableful of happy celebrants at the dinner and *below,* four proud chefs display their desserts, an ...ay which shattered many a dietary resolve.

1

4

1

Feminine pulchritude was always an essential ingredient of every carnival; this trio decorated one of the last shows.

2

Nursery stories, folk tales, popular songs, classics served as inspiration for routines or "courts" in the yearly programs.

3

Everybody's heart warms to the sight of a youngster and the junior section of the club was often the show's greatest hit.

4

Carnival was often a skater's first chance to skate in public. At least two dominion champions came out of this early 30s act.

5

Nancy Bruton chats with the first flower child, Ferdinand the Bull otherwise recognized as Peggy and Jane McCutcheon.

OPPOSITE PAGE, TOP
Wendy Griner, Bob Butterworth skate and mime a scene from the life of high society. Notice Miss Griner's robe, negligently thrown into her roadster as she waltzes away with the doorman.

BOTTOM
Three prancing, white reindeer enliven this year's program.

THIS PAGE, TOP
Wendy Griner, Greg Folk thrill audiences with dancing routines.

BOTTOM
Frances Dafoe won renown for herself and for the club as a skater but she was equally adept as a costume designer for carnival productions. Two of her sketches are reproduced below. *Extreme right* is shown a photograph of a penguin constructed from her design and the three reindeer *(opposite)* took shape from her sketch.

I t had been an autumn to remember. Days of burnished copper, bright with warmth and promise, followed each other in what seemed an endless procession. Occasionally, a wind with something bitter cruel in its breath, curled in from the lake. But the sun remained high, warm, dappling the waters of Toronto Bay with dancing highlights.

The nights were cool—cold, even. Frost turned the leaves of the maples and left crystalline fingers of ice trimming the water in the rain barrel. The weather—so pleasant for humans—had spoken harshly to the birds; the ducks and Canada geese had passed, headed for a land where weather muttered in more soothing tones.

Then came a day when the sun did not return. Grey cloud blanketed the sky; wispy strands of cloud, lower than the rest, scudded along pursued by chilling winds. Sparrows, the only wildlife brave enough to show itself, crouched intimidated on barren branches, their shoulder feathers puffed up like mufflers.

Winter gripped the town.

No more garish sunsets; night came as a sullen absence of light. Early in the month it snowed twice but both falls had disappeared within a day. For weeks it had been cold enough to snow but none had fallen. Now, in late November, the weather turned its attention to winter in earnest. The mercury balanced uneasily a few points above the Fahrenheit zero.

John O. Heward stepped from his home on John Street and adjusted his hat. He walked south to Front Street and then east along the lake front. From the lake came a cutting wind that sliced through greatcoat and muffler. Heward's breath caught in his chest, an icicle stabbing his lungs.

He crossed the street and walked carefully down the few frozen yards to the water's edge. The surface of the bay, all but a few feet inshore where listless rolls of waves stirred the water, was covered with a thin film of ice. Within weeks, Heward knew, it would be thick enough for curling. He smiled to himself, pulled his muffler tighter, and strode along the street to his office.

It is 1858 and the Toronto Curling Club has been in operation for more than twenty years. Heward is one of its mainstays, a hearty and reliable curler, steady in the tight spots.

Heward is a cricketer as well, a guiding light in the Toronto Cricket Club. In describing the season of 1857, the editor of *The Canadian Cricketer's Guide* described him as "the luckiest bat in Canada, and for many years unquestionably the most successful; still scores well, though not so heavily as ten or a dozen years ago. We have before us a book which furnishes such items to his credit as these:- 58, 56, 58, 39, 74 (n.o.), 45, 67 (n.o.), 58 &c. In the Canada match [vs US], Mr. H. obtained the highest score." The same publication shows that for the season Heward averaged twelve runs per inning over a series of ten matches, eighteen innings.

*   *   *

CHAPTER FIVE

The Gift of the Scots

119

The frozen surfaces of the Don River and Toronto Bay were used by curlers in the earliest years of the nineteenth century, but if the players organized into clubs, no evidence remains. The game came to Canada – as might be expected – as part of the baggage of emigrating Scots.

Until 1815 when the Duke of Wellington irrevocably smashed the imperial plans of Napoleon Bonaparte at Waterloo, most able-bodied Britons were held in military service. Following Waterloo, a massive economic depression gripped Great Britain and, with the compulsion of military service removed, many Scots emigrated to Canada. So many Scottish families swarmed to the province that, as W.A. Creelman says in *Curling, Past and Present*, "curling, like Jill, came tumbling after."

Few of the immigrants brought their stones. But that was a small deterrent. They gathered water-tumbled rocks from stream beds and lakeshores; the more inventive fitted their rocks with handles, others used the stones in a fashion that combined the roll of the bowler's delivery with the curler's slide. Others made do with six-inch slices of wood from a felled oak, maple, or birch; peeled and polished they made acceptable substitutes for Ailsa Craig granite. Some curlers drilled the wooden "stones" to accept poured lead for weight; others fitted them with metal hubs from wagon wheels.

(In Montreal – and in Quebec generally – cast-iron "stones" came into early use. The Montreal Curling Club, formed in 1807, continued to play with irons for many years and the difference in stones between the Quebec and Ontario curlers severely hampered competition between them.)

The Scots of Scarborough Township were probably the first in the Toronto district to curl. James Bicket, secretary of the Toronto Curling Club in 1840, and author of *The Canadian Curler's Manual*, the first North American publication on the game, says:

> Although the game has been played at Toronto, every winter, since 1829, it was never enjoyed to the same extent as it has been since the formation of the Club in 1836.

George Morton describes the scene:

> About Christmas time, when the ice was strong enough, a rink, maybe two, would be cleared of snow on the broad congealed surface of the bay; and out beyond the wharves could be seen upon the ice in all temperatures burly enthusiasts flinging the stone and plying the broom, with lusty shouts of encouragement, defiance, and an occasional dance for joy.

However, even before 1836 the Toronto curlers were sufficiently well organized to challenge their Scarborough brethren to a friendly game or two. One, the record of which has survived, took place in the winter of 1835-6 (although several observers of earlier years left recollections in which they recalled similar contests being played in the winters of 1832 and 1833).

In the 1835-6 game, a challenge was offered the Scarborough curlers by "the Toronto Club". The reference seems plain enough; some kind of organization – loosely defined, with few rules and possibly no officers – existed before the act of formalizing a club took place.

At any rate, the Toronto curlers issued a challenge. When it was received in Scarborough, the suburban Scots held a playoff to select the rink to compete. The younger members of the "club"—like its Toronto competition, not organized as such—challenged the more experienced elders. Calling themselves the "Auld Gang Siccars", the old timers consisted of James Findlay, Robert Hamilton, Thomas Brown, Abraham Torrance, Archibald Glendinning, James Gibson Sr, Andrew Fleming, with John Torrance as skip. The younger men, the "Wully Draigles", were Walter Miller, James McCowan, John Stobo, James Green, John Gibson, Robert Scott, James Weir, and James Gibson, skip. It was still in the day of eight men per side, each man with one stone per end.

It was one occasion on which youth paid off against maturity; the Draigles won by eight shots.

The same rink of Scarborough "youngsters" then journeyed to Toronto and the game with the local club was played on Toronto Bay ice near the foot of Church Street. The contingents and their scores:

Everywhere there was a sheet of ice sufficiently large, Toronto curlers took advantage of it to celebrate the ancient game of the Scots. On the frozen surface of the lake in High Park, this band of early sportsmen gathered; the date of the sketch is not shown. Note the basket of bottled refreshments resting against the tree trunk, *right foreground.*

TORONTO	SCARBOROUGH
Dr Telfer	Walter Miller
Alexander Ogilvie	James McCowan
William Henderson	John Stobo
Alexander Badenach	James Green
John O. Heward	John Gibson
Honourable Justice Morrison	Robert Scott
George Denholm	James Weir
Captain Thomas Dick, skip-16	James Gibson, skip-31

The Scarborough-Toronto matches continued throughout the winter, the players taking sleighs or occasionally hiking to the host rink. "Many an early curler," remarks historian Edwin C. Guillet, "is said to have set out the night before and travelled all night on 'Shank's mare', curled all the next day, and returned home thereafter."

As often as not, the formation of clubs was prompted by the need to standardize the rules of play. The length of play, for instance, was variable from region to region. In Scotland, where weather conditions made the season most unreliable, curling was usually an all-day affair; lunch was brought and the game continued as long as light lasted. In Canada, with weather conditions somewhat more reliable, time limits were usually fixed on game; the records of early matches are studded with references to "... at the end of three hours", "... after four hours' hard play." Very early in its career, the TCC adopted a plan whereby the first team to achieve a certain score–7, 13, 21, 31–was declared the winner.

In the winter after its founding, the Toronto club adopted the procedure that before playing, the members lined up in military fashion and counted off from left to right. Bicket, secretary of the club, explained the regimen by saying:

> The player who makes a mistake [that is, plays out of order] is fit neither for a curler nor a soldier. This method has been practised at Toronto, since the winter of 1837-1838–when military terms and ideas were infused into every department of life.

Bicket's mention of the military is a reference to the short but disruptive rebellion of William Lyon Mackenzie's followers during which large numbers of Toronto men were pressed into service with the militia.

The standardization of playing rules was certainly one of the prime reasons for the formation of the club in Toronto. But a secondary reason of no little importance was the question posed before every game: Who is to clear the ice?

As yet, there were no shed roofs built to protect the ice surface from new-fallen snow. Every game was preceded by the tedious task of shovelling clear the space between the hacks, and it was "wasted" time the curlers resented. Bicket says:

> By the judicious arrangement of the managers, in appointing the hours of playing, and in having the ice ready before the curlers meet, the time which was formerly wasted in preparations that may be performed by laborers, is now spent in the game; and thus the recre-

JOSEPH W. LESLIE
President
Toronto Curling Club
1896-7

ation can be shared by many, who should otherwise, by the nature of their occupations, be excluded from the rink.

When the Toronto Curling Club was formed, Upper Canada was a two-fisted, hard-drinking colony. Few tasks were undertaken without liberal lashings of booze and the game of curling was no exception. In 1840 Bicket skirted the issue, saying only, "Intoxication on the ice is…unknown among *good* players." (Emphasis supplied.) In the 1876 *Annual* of the Ontario Curling Association one writer said:

> Many people are under the impression that whisky and curling go hand in hand. This was the case at one time, but I rejoice to say that bottles of whisky at the head of each rink during play is now the exception and not the rule.

Still, in the same *Annual* appeared an engraving showing the famous "Red Jackets" rink of the TCC in play on its old stamping grounds, Toronto Bay. There, in the lower-right corner of the picture, is a basket well stocked with bottled sustenance.

The same engraving ran in the OCA *Annual* for several years – the Red Jackets were a continuing phenomenon – but by 1879, the editor, probably cognizant of the increasing pressures of the temperance movement, draped a black cloth across the basket to conceal the bounty within.

The Toronto *Examiner* of 11 March 1840 details the play of four rinks from the TCC, two rinks each of bachelors against two of married men. The result – a draw – salved the feelings of both married men and singles; neither state was obviously superior so far as curling was concerned. For the record, the results read:

"As a rink the 'Red Jackets' achieved a record which has rarely, if ever, been matched. They won laurels, not only at home in Ontario but at Montreal, Buffalo, Detroit and other distant places. And, wherever they went they advertised curling as supreme among winter sports and left the impression that the curlers of Ontario were not only the best players of the game but the best of fellows. Therefore the fame of the 'Red Jackets' rink is secure for all time."

JOHN STEVENSON,
Curling in Ontario.

RINK NO. 1

Married	Single
A. Badenach	R. Creighton
J. Watson	John Leys
J. Walker	William Ross
— Jennings	R.G. Anderson
A. Kinneard	Alfred Stone
R. McClure	John Maitland
William Struthers	Montagu Kelly
Alexander Rosland, skip-19	George Denholm, skip-21

RINK NO. 2

Married	Single
John Thompson	Samuel Spreull
William Reynolds	Joseph Morrison
James Bell	James Dick
William Thompson	Thomas Ewart
Thomas Dick	S.B. Campbell
J. Murchison	Angus Morrison
J.W. Brent	J. McMurrich
James Beckett, skip-19	George P. Dickson, skip-17

As already mentioned, curling in the early years was limited to competitions between nearby clubs. Transportation was, in many cases, primitive, or non-existent in most. In *Curling in Ontario*, John A. Stevenson writes of this era:

> Visiting teams, unless each member of them had the strength of Hercules, could not carry for any long distance their stones as well as their besoms and shovels which were an indispensable part of their equipment for removing snow... Members of the Toronto C.C. and Hamilton Thistles whose homes were only some fifty miles apart, had to allow three days for playing a match in the other city—one day for the outward journey, one for the match, and one for travelling home.... However, Toronto and Scarborough clubs were so close to one another that they were in the habit of playing matches every few weeks while the frost lasted.

In 1856 the Grand Trunk was opened between Toronto and Montreal, and the Great Western had started to inch its way west from the city. The new means of getting about solved most of the problems which had, so far, restricted curling. The time required for a game was shortened, the journey between points was made in warmth and relative comfort, and one's stones and brooms no longer seemed such a ponderous burden.

In spite of the problems of travels, bonspiels had been popular in the earliest days. Bicket mentions one between Scarborough and Toronto rinks. "They played at Toronto, on 12th February last [1839], with twenty-four players aside, when their Excellencies the Governor General [Lord Sydenham] and the Lieutenant Governor [Sir George Arthur] were spectators of the game." But after the railways had been completed, the phenomenon of bonspiels mushroomed. In 1858 the first of the mammoth bonspiels was held but the record is scanty. The *Annual* of 1876 says only:

> In February of 1858, there was a bonspiel played on Burlington Bay—East *vs.* West. There were 16 rinks a side and the score was, East 384, West, 398—majority for the West 14 shots. A similar bonspiel was played on the River Don, February 9, 1859, 21 rinks a side. The score was East 451, West 533, majority for West 82 shots.
>
> There was a bonspiel played on Burlington Bay about the year 1863, of which we have no record.

(There is much vagueness about the origin of the word "bonspiel". Various authorities trace it to almost every language of modern Europe; the most reasonable explanation seems to be that it derives from the Danish, *bondespil*, "a country game".)

Sometime about 1865, the Toronto Curling Club acquired its first indoor rink. In a deal effected with the Yorkville Skating Rink, TCC members were granted practice and play time on the Yorkville ice. The rink was located in the Clover Hill section of Yonge Street between Wellesley and College Streets, on the northwest corner of today's Irwin Street. (The small rise for which the district was named has long since disappeared in street levellings.)

Ontario curlers waged a long, and eventually successful, battle for reduced fares on the railways when bonspiels were to be attended. In 1883 most major railroads cut round-trip fares for curlers to one and one-third the cost of a single ticket; in 1885 a further concession of a flat two-cents-per-mile fare assisted those clubs which wanted to make circle trips to visit several opponents.

It is a measure of the city's growth that the Yorkville rink, located in what we today would call the midtown – or even *down*town – section of the city, was *outside* the city in the suburban village of Yorkville. At the time, Toronto's population was some fifty thousand persons.

If a photograph was ever made, or a sketch drawn, of the Yorkville rink no trace of it remains. We can assume that it was a complete building – that is, more than just a shed – that protected the curlers from not only snowfall but the sharp winds of winter as well. If they were lucky, those early curlers may have enjoyed also the luxury of a heated changing room.

The Yorkville rink filled the needs of the TCC for ten years; in 1875 the club moved its activities to the lumber yard belonging to J.P. Wagner located on the block between Adelaide and King Streets, just west of Bay Street. Again, details are lacking, but it is reasonable to guess that the Wagner rink was covered with a shed only; such sheds were common structures in early lumber yards, and were used primarily to protect new wood from the elements while it was air-cured.

In any case, the Toronto Curling Club was, by 1875, committed to building its own rink – the first built for and owned by the club.

The new rink was located on the north side of Adelaide Street West, midway between Peter and John Streets, directly opposite a street known then and now as Widmer Street. The club opened the building, for the purposes of curling, at least, on 28 December 1876, although the formal opening was delayed for a couple of weeks until the Governor General, Lord Dufferin, could preside at the occasion. It was, said the newspapers of the time, "the first covered rink erected in Ontario for curling," "a palatial covered rink."

The Grand Trunk Railway, shown here crossing the Niagara gorge on its two-deck bridge, was used by Toronto curlers to get to bonspiels.

125

The Governor General, Lord Dufferin (*top*, with broom handle held horizontally off the ice), curls with a party of friends at Rideau Hall, Ottawa. In the 1870s, the Earl and Countess Dufferin were enthusiastic supporters of curling and skating.

In a book published by the Ontario Curling Association in 1950, John A. Stevenson describes the event:

> Senator (later Sir D.L.) Macpherson the Patron of the Club, presented Lord Dufferin with a fine pair of Ailsa Craig curling stones, which had his name inscribed on their handles and Mr. [Angus] Morrison, the Mayor of Toronto, offered the city's tribute in the form of a fine besom, whose handle was encircled with a silver band with Lord Dufferin's name, surmounted by a silver beaver and maple leaf, engraved on it. Lady Dufferin . . . received a beautiful pair of gold and silver plated skates, which Mr. David Walker presented. . . . Lord Dufferin . . . skipped a Viceregal rink against a very strong rink picked by the President of the club, which won rather decisively by thirty shots to seventeen.

David Walker, who presented the skates to Lady Dufferin, was a well-known member of the TCC, the proprietor of the Walker House hotel at York and Front Streets, and one of a quartet whose prowess at curling had made the game (in this age of the first transatlantic cable) a front-page story in newspapers around the world.

In 1864, the Toronto club, flushed with many local victories and confident of its supremacy, issued a challenge to the Buffalo Caledonia Curling Club. The Buffalo curlers were entertained in Toronto and, on 19 February 1864, repaid the compliment, playing host to the Toronto club. An even more important result was the introduction the following year of the great international bonspiel at Black Rock near Buffalo.

The Americans, twenty-three rinks strong, were represented by curlers from New York, Ohio, New Jersey, and Pennsylvania. In addition to the Toronto club, Canadian curlers assembled from Paris, Sarnia, Peterborough, and Ayr.

One of the TCC rinks had dubbed itself "Her Majesty's Rink", whether by royal permission or merely in a joyous burst of royalist sentiment is uncertain. The members of the rink clothed themselves in scarlet jackets, which prompted their opponents at Buffalo to adopt the stars and stripes as sweater adornments and to take the name, the "President's Rink". The Americans dubbed their Canadian competitors the "Red Jackets"; it was an appropriate designation and clung as an identifying label for twelve years.

The original members of the Red Jackets were John Shedden, skip, J.E. Thomson as lead, George Ewart as second, and Captain Charles Perry as third.

For the 1865 Black Rock bonspiel the personnel were Shedden, Thomson, Major Gray, and Perry. Within months, Thomas McGaw took Thomson's place and the rink's members remained constant for a few years. The final change was occasioned by the arrival in Toronto of Walker, about to make his Queen City reputation as a *hôtelier* as he had in Chatham. He joined the rink as third, Shedden retired, and Perry became skip.

The bonspiel at Black Rock brought curling into the front parlours of millions of homes in the United States and Canada. Never before had the excitement of the sport been brought home to non-curlers in so dra-

Curling swept the settled parts of Canada in the 1880s and 1890s and by 1900 had become the country's most popular sport. So determined had the competition become, so fierce the rivalry for prizes, that the executive committee of the Ontario Curling Association " . . . expressed strongly the view that the practice of playing for trophies and prizes has been now carried to dangerous lengths and was transforming the game of curling from a friendly rivalry . . . into fierce struggles for victory."

matic a style. And it was the further exploits of the Red Jackets that kept curling on page one.

From 1871 through 1877 the rink reigned supreme; it demolished opposition in both Canada and the United States. John A. Stevenson, writing of the rink, says:

> All four were highly expert curlers, each playing the position best suited to him. Perry, after ten years as third, became skip and Walker, who was rated a fine skip, thought it no slur upon his skill to play for ten years as third. For the same length of time McGaw played as lead and Gray as second. The quartette played as a thoroughly harmonious team, reposing complete confidence in the ability and judgment of their skip and in the skill and loyalty of each other. They did not regard any position in the rink as superior or inferior and they were incapable of jealousy of one another. Canada has never known a better blended combination of curlers and they reinforced their notable skill as players with an expert mastery of strategic wiles, never hesitating to employ them with a deft touch when they were playing opponents liable to prove easy victims of such wiles.

Even with its new Adelaide Street rink, the Toronto club continued to play on Toronto Bay until well into the 1880s.

The demand for ice often outstripped the club's ability to provide inside sheets. In the latter days, the favourite locale was near the foot of Bay Street; on the north side of Front Street, where the Royal York Hotel stands today, an unused boathouse served as a storage shed for stones, brooms, and other equipment.

The decision to build the Huron Street rink seems to have marked the end of outdoor curling. From 1887, when the Huron rink was completed, until the present, we find no further references to curling activity on the bay.

The initial push to move from Adelaide Street was size; the club had grown in membership and there was simply not enough ice to provide space for those who wanted—demanded!—to curl. The Huron Street building doubled the space from four to eight rinks. A curler of the time described the facilities in these words:

> The most sumptuously housed is the Victoria Club in which the time-honoured Toronto Club is accommodated. It has eight rinks under the cover of two sheds, very nice and modern billiard rooms and card rooms and a lawn which provides eight or ten bowling rinks.... in summer all the intermediate space between our two brick sheds, an angle of grass, aglow at the edges with flowers, the wooden fence at the east end lustrous with grapes and a mass of shade, the tennis players in their flannels, the bowlers in their shirt-sleeves and Glasgow-made bowls everywhere.

It is the first mention of lawn bowling and tennis directly associated with one of the constituent clubs of the TCSCC. (In the 1840s, it will be remembered, both bowling and tennis were indirectly connected with the Toronto Cricket Club; both sports were played at the Caer Howell Hotel on University Avenue, a hotel which functioned as the informal social centre for the cricketers.)

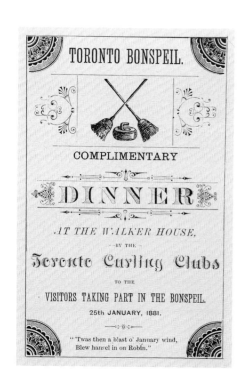

TORONTO BONSPEIL.

COMPLIMENTARY

DINNER

AT THE WALKER HOUSE,
— BY THE —

Toronto Curling Clubs

TO THE

VISITORS TAKING PART IN THE BONSPEIL.

25th JANUARY, 1881.

"'Twas then a blast o' January wind,
Blew hansel in on Robin."

In 1895 the Royal Caledonia Club of Scotland, the mother club of world curling, had approved women for membership. About 1900 the first Canadian women's club, in Montreal, was admitted to membership and in 1910 a gallant band of some thirty-five women formed the Ladies Toronto Curling Club under the wing of the Toronto Curling Club. By 1913 the ladies' club had been admitted to Ontario Curling Association membership. Apart from some fall off of activity in the war years, the ladies' section has remained an active and lively organization.

In 1925 the Toronto club installed a refrigeration plant and started to manufacture its own ice. The Toronto club was the first to take the momentous step: For the first time club members were assured of six months' competition regardless of the weather. "February thaws" which had cancelled many a bonspiel in the past were no longer disastrous occurrences.

Finally, in 1938, members of the Toronto Curling Club took the step which put world curlers in their debt for all time: The club introduced curling stones standardized as to size, weight, and other characteristics and decreed that matched sets of the stones, belonging to the club, would be made available to members and visitors alike for bonspiels played on club premises.

Again, it was a step of organizational genius. All sport depends on near-identical conditions prevailing for all competitors. With two strokes – artificial indoor ice and matched stones – the Toronto club rationalized a sport badly in need of firmer guidelines.

Very little in Canadian life remained "normal" during the war years, 1939-45. Family life was uprooted and every aspect of human endeavour was altered, often beyond recognition. The orderly progression of friendly curling matches and bonspiels disappeared and, as did most sports, curling went into hibernation for the duration of hostilities. By the early fifties life had largely returned to normal and curling revived along with other aspects of Canadian life. By the mid-fifties almost all curling clubs – the Toronto Curling Club most certainly – had long waiting lists of would-be curlers.

In 1958 the six sheets of ice in the new TCSCC clubhouse were ready for games and bonspiels, and the game flourished. All six sheets of ice were in constant use and it is fair to say that by 1960 the level of activity had reached a new peak.

During the summer months the curling sheets are rented to skaters, but for the rest of the year the curlers keep all six sheets occupied.

In mid-season, during the curling year 1969-70, what became known as an "astonishing deterioration" took place on sheet five. The ice surface heaved, warped, bent, and twisted in such un-curling like fashion that some skips found they had to place their brooms on sheets four or six to guide a teammate's rock into the house on five.

Curlers are said to be perfectionists and they are also, generally speaking, vocal. In this instance they certainly communicated their distress to the board of directors which appointed a committee to study the problem. And, none too soon, because now all the other sheets were beginning to be affected, in greater or lesser degree, with the same "astonishing deterioration."

Some curling clubs in the eastern part of Canada West or Ontario – those clubs in most immediate contact with the iron-playing clubs of Quebec – often saw merit in the iron stones and adopted them instead of granite. In cold weather, and under cover, the irons were superb; but when the weather moderated, or when a strong sun warmed the irons, they melted the ice, and left the teehead pitted with hollow depressions.

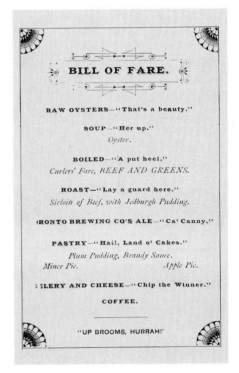

BILL OF FARE.

RAW OYSTERS – "That's a beauty."

SOUP – "Her up."
Oyster.

BOILED – "A put heel."
Curlers' Fare, BEEF AND GREENS.

ROAST – "Lay a guard here."
Sirloin of Beef, with Jedburgh Pudding.

TORONTO BREWING CO'S ALE – "Ca' Canny."

PASTRY – "Hail, Land o' Cakes."
Plum Pudding, Brandy Sauce.
Mince Pie.   Apple Pie.

CELERY AND CHEESE – "Chip the Winner."

COFFEE.

"UP BROOMS, HURRAH!"

The committee hired a firm of consulting engineers which immediately ran some soil tests on the ground beneath ice sheet five and others. The engineers found that the soil was frozen, in some places to a depth of as much as sixteen feet. Sixteen feet of permafrost! It was the slow but inexorable movement of this huge mass of frozen soil that caused the curling sheets to heave and buckle. And it was the uninterrupted twelve-month use of the rinks that permitted the permafrost to penetrate so deeply. The solution to the problem was simplicity itself: After the curling season is concluded, and before the ice is rented to the skaters, warm brine is circulated through the refrigeration pipes. The frozen ground is thus thawed before the ice is prepared for the skaters.

During the many meetings and discussions about the curling-ice problem it became obvious that the club was short of one important staff member – an icemaker. The ice required for both curling and skating had been, from the opening of the new club, the responsibility of the staff engineers. In the meantime, the search for a competitive edge had brought to icemaking a sophistication that required a specialist. Many curling clubs had added an icemaker to their staffs and now, the TCSCC joined their ranks.

Good management and good luck often go hand-in-hand. In this case they certainly did. As its first icemaker the club hired Donald C. Campbell, a member of the famous Campbell rink of Saskatchewan which won the Canadian championship in 1955 and drew seconds in 1954 and 1957. Campbell, a former member of the RCMP, has been club icemaker since 1972 and the ice in all that time has been superb.

Since the establishment of the Governor General's Trophy in 1894 as emblematic of curling supremacy in Ontario, the club has won it seven times in 1904, 1925, 1927, 1929, 1934, 1936, and 1938.

The fellowship among curlers is warm and the competition is keen. It is exciting to trace the history of curling within the club during the past 150 years, and to note that the ancient game of curling has been brought to Canada from Scotland and has been successfully handed on to the youngsters of the 1970s.

ALL IN THE HOUSE

The "Red Jackets," the most famous rink to issue from the Toronto Curling Club – or, indeed, from any Canadian club – is shown at work on the Don River in Toronto in 1870. The skip is Captain Charles Perry *(No. 4, kneeling at left)*. Thomas McGraw, No. 8, proprietor of the Queen's Hotel, was lead. Major Gray, No. 6, was second and David Walker, No. 7, later to found the Walker House Hotel, was third. An expert curler, looking at this picture, said: "It appears like a good end for the stones are all in the house." In other reproductions of this sketch the basket peeking into the right corner is shown in full and is, itself, full – of Scotch.

Remember when they told us about the "good old days"?

"Way back then, son . . ." the curling situation was pretty lousy, if the truth be known. During the first world war, soldiers (note two in uniform) and civilians alike turned out to shovel a patch of ice on Toronto Bay so they could play a few ends before the daylight faded. Several shovel handles protrude from the snow banks.

OFFICIAL OPENING OF THE TOR...

RLING CLUB, NOV. 18th 1938.

1

The introduction of matched stones, a move initiated by the Toronto Curling Club in 1938, did more than anything else to standardize, and eventually popularize, the sport.

2

The Hamilton-Toronto rivalry has long been a fixture in the club. Four rinks from each club pose for a photograph taken before the start of the 1948 edition of the battle.

3

During the 1948 season this rink from the Toronto Curling Club competed for and won the Ryrie-Ellis-Birks-Trophy in the Ontario Curling Bonspiel. *From the left* Frank Smith, Tom Beattie (holding trophy), Mel Cunnington, and Bill Wyse.

3

1

1   This happy quartet won the Robertson in 1953. *Rear,* Ethel Hugill and Nancy Palmer, *front,* Edith Creswicke and Flo Seawright.

2   In 1957, the first year of competition for the Cecilia Glass Trophy, this rink from the Toronto club won the award at Weston. Mrs J.C. Malcolmson, skip, holds the trophy. *From the right,* Mrs J.H. Mandsley, Mrs R.C. Avery and Mrs G.W. Wells.

3   *From the top,* M. MacNaughton, Loraine Ostler, Hilda Cail, and Nan McPhun were 1964 winners of the Malcolmson Trophy.

4   In 1958 this rink of Scottish ladies toured Canada and the United States. In Toronto they met this quartet from the TCSCC. *From the left, front row,* Mrs J.C. Malcolmson, Edith Creswicke, Mrs H.R. Knowles, Mrs J.H. McIlroy.

5   Best record posted to date for any TCSCC rink was established in 1967 by this rink skipped by Neva Paul. The women were runners up in the Ontario Ladies Curling Association Silver "D" competition. *From the left,* Laura Erwin, Gwenneth Goodman, Neva Paul, Isabel Lutton.

4

5

1

2

3

4

1

Top row, Len Smith, Bill Wyse, and *front row*, Harold Field and Jim Knox comprised one TCSCC rink of recent years.

2

Top row, Bill Wyse, Jim Knox, and *front row*, Harold Field and Strachan Bongard show how the personnel of rinks change.

3

From the top, Tom Beattie, Bill Wyse, Harry Stronach and Gordon Brydson were another quartet of recent vintage.

4

From the left, Bill Wyse with Reg Lockhart, Doug McVittie and George Gardhouse comprised yet another of the club's rinks.

As we have seen, the Toronto Cricket Club, from the earliest years of the 1840s, was closely linked with facilities for both lawn bowling and tennis. The association was physical, not organizational; there is nothing to suggest that the proximity of the cricket pitch, bowling green, and tennis court was anything more than a happy coincidence. Coincidence it may have been in the beginning, but the coincidence gradually became habit and habit grew into tradition. Today, a century and more later, the lawn bowling and racquet sections of the TCSCC constitute three of its most vigorous components.

Sometime in or about 1840 the Toronto Cricket Club established its first permanent home at the Taddle, near the corner of College and McCaul Streets, on a corner of the W.H. Boulton estate. Next to the cricket grounds to the east was located the posh resort hotel, Caer Howell, the former home of Chief Justice William Dummer Powell on the corner of College Street and University Avenue. Today, the corner is considered a mere step from the heart of the business section but in the early nineteenth century it was thought to be a sufficient distance from the city to serve as a retreat from city cares. The Caer Howell Hotel served the well-to-do families of Toronto as a semi-rural retreat from city life, where business cares could be forgotten for a few days of relaxation. Businessmen, merchants, doctors, lawyers, government officials journeyed with their families to the Caer Howell to spend a weekend free from the frantic pace of city life.

It was, of course, from the same group of men that the Toronto Cricket Club drew most of its members. The population of the city was small and the number of men whose work allowed them free time to play cricket was smaller still. When Boulton offered a corner of his St Leger racetrack as space for a cricket pitch he did so in full awareness that many – perhaps most – of those who would play on the property were well acquainted with the grounds through their sojourns at the Caer Howell.

During the midgame break in cricket, maids from the hotel served tea to players and spectators; after the game everyone adjourned to the hotel bar where the game was replayed over drinks. The catering service supplied by the hotel suggests that those requesting it were valued customers, as indeed they were. In the earliest years the cricketers played regularly on Wednesday but the hotel proprietor could assume that a goodly number of the home team, as well as some of the spectators, would show up at Caer Howell on the following Saturday as his weekend guests.

For the amusement of his guests, the hotel's owner had installed a bowling green and a sunken tennis court on the front lawn. (What advantage a sunken tennis court offered, other than novelty, is never made clear.) Wednesday's cricketers were Sunday bowlers and tennis players – there can be no doubt about it. By the 1870s the association had become more formal; when the Toronto club played host to touring English cricketers the membership of the bowling club was invited to attend the formal dinner.

CHAPTER SIX

On Bowling Green and Racquet Courts

"A well-known humorist of the cricket field in those days was Wooten, the brawny host of Caer Howell, and the interchange of chaff between him and J.O. Heward was often of the raciest. G.A. Barber, too, brought a cheery laugh into the game, as well as a highly trained and very sensitive knowledge of it, and he more than anybody taught the young idea how to shoot."

T.C. PATTESON
in
Sixty Years of Canadian Cricket

Studying the lay of the land.

A battle in the forecourts.

Gentlemen, the pleasure is ours;
better luck next time.

We have no records of what happened to the bowling club that had been invited to the cricketers' dinner, but in less than a decade the Victoria Skating and Curling Association had built a fine, new home on Huron Street for the Toronto Curling Club and soon bowling greens were incorporated as part of its grounds.

Lawn bowling and curling go together as a natural pair; each requires similar skills—sharpness of eye, judgment of distances, ability to compete as a member of a team. In addition, each sport provides an off-season use of the club; combining the two sports under one roof means, in effect, that there is no off season.

Over the years the bowling section of the curling club was usually the junior section in terms of number of members but, as often as not, the leader in terms of spirit and enthusiasm.

Much later, probably about 1926 a small but active lawn bowling section was affiliated with the Toronto Cricket Club. The new section appeared at about the time the club moved to its new Armour Heights home on Wilson Avenue. The reason lawn bowling came to the fore at this moment seems rather obvious—for the first time the club had its own property, and plenty of it, and improvements to the property (such as the building and maintenance of bowling greens) improved one's own land, not the landlord's. At best, the cricket club's lawn bowling section never numbered more than "about twenty men, few in number but mighty keen bowlers," as one former member recollects.

At the amalgamation of the clubs in 1957 the two lawn bowling sections merged—and immediately became inactive for almost two years.

"The Davis Cup was being played that year at the new TCSCC grounds," a lawn bowler with an evergreen memory recalls. "Davis Cup play, that year, was on grass courts and the committee had taken over the bowling greens that were on the site and incorporated them as part of the tennis courts. After the cup play was over it took us nearly two years to get our bowling greens back. Two years!" (A note of outrage creeps into his voice at this point.) "But justice prevailed. It took time, but justice prevailed."

As it is with lawn bowling, so it is with tennis: The earliest years are obscured. We know that shortly after the Toronto Curling Club opened its new clubhouse on Huron Street tennis courts were in place and being used (see page 28). Of the intervening years, of the Caer Howell influence, we know nothing.

Tennis became an exceedingly popular sport at the curling club and former members of the club remember the intricate negotiations required to bargain for court time more appropriate to one's timetable.

The modern game of tennis had been invented in 1873 by an English gentleman sick to death with endless rounds of croquet. He called his invention "sphairistike" after an ancient Greek ball game and, naturally, the unwieldy name was popularly shortened to "sticky". To retain some dignity its inventor rechristened it "lawn tennis" to distinguish it from the older game that was played indoors. By 1879 the Montreal Lawn Tennis Club was in full operation, and in 1883, four years before the curling club's new clubhouse was finished, a Toronto club was advertising for entrants to a mixed doubles competition. (It is interesting to speculate that the 1883 club was also associated with the curlers although the curling rink of the time, on Adelaide Street, had no courts.) Ladies' championships were held in 1891 under the sponsorship of the Canadian Lawn Tennis Association. From the beginning tennis had been popular with ladies; it was a sport that could be played genteely in floor-length skirts and voluminous blouses.

So far as we can tell, the cricket club had no facilities for tennis (Caer Howell excepted) until 1926 when it moved to Amour Heights. Sometime after that date grass and clay courts were constructed, and by the time of amalgamation in 1958, the Toronto Cricket Club tennis section was as active – if not as old – as that in the Toronto Curling Club.

Between the two dates, 1926 and 1958, the club built eleven courts – six clay, two grass, and three *en tout cas*. Today ten green-surfaced Har-Tru courts are in almost constant action, night and day, during summer weather.

Summer weather... a telling phrase. Tennis and weather are – or have been – inseparable.

In recent years the highly publicized tournaments of touring professional tennis players have made the sport popular beyond accommodation; public courts in some cities are in use twenty-four hours a day during good weather. Still, Canada has produced few players of first rank; the best, past and present, are few in number. One main reason is the country's atrocious weather.

While winter provides the conditions under which Canada produces a Kathy Kreiner, the same conditions do not help at all if one hopes to produce a Chris Evert. Once, when asked what Canadian tennis players could do to improve their game, Rod Laver answered, "Leave the country."

It might have been good advice at one time but technology has rendered it obsolete. In winter weather the club erects the "bubble" and four courts are converted from part-time to full-time use. As anyone who has tried to book court time can attest, tennis is just as popular in March as it is in July.

Faye Urban of the club has held the Canadian ladies championship and Peter Burwash was Canadian champion in 1971.

The only "new" sport that has surfaced since the amalgamation of the three constituent clubs is squash. There is no indication that it was ever played at any one of the original clubs. In a very real sense, the game, and the courts for playing it, are an accidental addition to the roster of TCSCC sports. A member, primarily a curler but possessed of a vicious forehand smash as well, tells the story:

The amalgamation of the clubs had proceeded smoothly and we were now busy planning for the new clubhouse on Wilson Avenue. At every meeting of the building committee somebody would suggest that we *double* the size of the men's locker room, *enlarge* the dining room, make the bar *bigger*. All our discussions seemed to be in the directions of making the clubhouse bigger, grander.

I kept questioning the cost but we always seemed to have enough money. Finally, one meeting it happened. After all the talk of mak-

GORDON ANDERSON
Canadian singles squash champ
Canadian doubles squash champ
1972-3

141

ing this bigger, enlarging that, someone spoke up and said, "Why don't we put in a squash court?" I'm sure he was being sarcastic.

Well, I kind of liked squash but more with the idea of showing some of the other committee members how dumb it was to always talk about making everything bigger, I spoke up and seconded the motion. Before I could catch my breath the committee voted to look into it, found we had the money and, by golly, we had two squash courts! If I'd known how easy it would be to get it through, I might have suggested building six.

Since the first two courts mentioned above, both singles courts, the club has added three more singles and one doubles to help meet the demand. Still, as with the other racquet sport, tennis, court time is in short supply and avidly sought.

Earlier in these pages we noted that it takes time to build champions; the Toronto Skating Club competed in Canadian championships for nineteen years before it placed a name on the winners' list. In terms of age, squash is a mere infant compared with the other club sports. Yet, it has already started making a name for the club.

Craig Benson, wearing club colours, was the first non-American to win the US junior championship; he captured the Canadian title as well.

Ian Shaw won the US title for an unprecedented three times.

Lorne G. Main also captured both US and Canadian junior titles.

Gordon Anderson has brought credit to the club every time he has stepped on court. For a new sport squash has been uncommonly productive of champions.

* * *

As has been stated, it is impossible to prove that tennis and lawn bowling were officially, organizationally connected with either of the early clubs. But connected they were through the men who played one or more of the sports. It comes as no surprise that as soon as the Toronto Cricket Club established its grounds at Amour Heights, on property of its own, tennis courts and bowling greens should share the space. And it is no more surprising that when the Victoria Club built its own clubhouse on Huron Street tennis courts and bowling greens should share its grounds.

The Nestea national junior championships of 1976 were almost a rout for the young tennis players of the TCSCC. Winners were, *from the left:* Terry Fahlenbrock, Dan Whittaker, Robert Gordon, Owen Pellew, Pat Sinclair, Susan Gillespie, Susan Dale.

HOW TO CELEBRATE

AN AFFECTIONATE LOOK AT THE TCSCC BY PHOTOGRAPHER JOHN DE VISSER

A 150TH BIRTHDAY

As 1976 ran short of time, and as 1977 was waiting for its allotted period in the limelight, the Toronto Cricket, Skating, and Curling Club was, as it and its constituent member clubs have always been, busy. *Very* busy.

As always,
now as in
the past, the
emphasis is
on tomorrow.

We will guide,
train, direct,
but, when the
time comes
that we must
release young
hands, we let
go in the
firm belief
that the next
steps will
be made in
full and easy
confidence.

This book is the first to set forth the separate and combined histories of the three Toronto sports clubs which form the Toronto Cricket, Skating, and Curling Club. It is far from being the first book, or the only book, which mentions the early clubs and their relationship to the city at large. Members interested in club history should read deeply, pensively, from the books listed in the bibliography which follows. Here, the reader will find a wealth of detail about the club, about its past and about its present. And, in a way, a "prediction" about its future.

The bibliography represents the books consulted which contributed *significantly* to the development of the present text. A larger list – perhaps double the length – could have been developed by including also those books read but not quoted within the text.

Every source touches on the accomplishments of one or another of the three clubs which amalgamated to form today's TCSCC. The references are often fleeting, more often extended. In total they represent an astonishing tribute to 150 years of participation in, and pursuit of excellence in sports in Toronto.

Since 1958 the combined histories of the Toronto Cricket Club, the Toronto Skating Club, and the Toronto Curling Club are too recent and well known to require detailed recapitulation. Additionally, recent history is difficult to assess; values shift, the bases on which lasting judgments can be made alter and change. Time – long chunks of time – are required before value assessments can be made with confidence.

One fact, one value judgment which *can* be made about the Toronto Cricket, Skating, and Curling Club, is that it has accomplished what must have seemed to the constituent memberships of 1957 a near-impossible feat: the unique contribution of each club to an amalgmated facility has been retained while a true union of purpose has been achieved.

On the surface, it sounds like a conundrum. The usual pattern, when two or more groups enter into a partnership, is for one to dominate, to impose on the new, larger organization a pattern of thought and behaviour that marks it unmistakably as Group *A*'s and not Group *B*'s.

Nonetheless, the TCSCC achieved the impossible. The special character and purpose which gave each organization its *raison d'être* as an individual club has been retained. Yet the total is greater than the sum of its parts.

It is an achievement of no little distinction. Much of the credit belongs to the combined memberships at the time of amalgamation; considerable thought was given to the possibility of factional problems and creative safeguards were devised to protect the new club against the occurrence. To cite but one example: In the first three years of its existence, the TCSCC presidency was rotated between members of the original three clubs with the vice-presidency denied to a member of the same original club as the president. This provision, and others like it, eased the transition between three dissimilar clubs into a unified organization pursuing the single goal of excellence in its chosen fields.

"When the club was first formed there was an awful lot of unhappiness about the name – the Toronto Cricket, Skating, and Curling Club. It seemed like a mouthful, and took forever to write when you were mailing your monthly cheque. Eventually, there was a general meeting called to get a new name, something shorter, easier to say.

"Well, the meeting dragged on and on. All kinds of new names were suggested and all of them turned down for one reason or another. By the time everyone was getting awfully tired of the exercise, a big voice spoke out from the back of the room.

"'Mr Chairman,' it said. Every head in the room turned to see the speaker – Colonel Clifford Sifton.

"'Mr Chairman, I move that the name of this club *be* and *remain* the Toronto Cricket, Skating, and Curling Club.'

"The walls shook with applause. With one stroke Clifford Sifton created a club."

MRS KAY SEVERS

Credit also is due to the membership of the club since amalgamation. Of each member, of each section, it has required a commitment to a common purpose in which individual preferences are submerged for the common good.

Which is *not* to say that a cricketer will be as happy on a curling sheet as he is on the cricket pitch, nor that a skater will be as satisfied practising a draw shot as he will be practising a salchow. The individual preferences remain.

The strength of the TCSCC remains that it clings tenaciously to diversity under the umbrella of a club loyalty that supercedes individual preferences.

"Prediction" of the future?

This only.

The future will be as the past has been – unpredictable. But, whatever the imponderables, one thing seems certain: The TCSCC will survive with undiminished vigour and enthusiasm.

Indeed there will be changes; life itself is constant change. Individuals and organizations adapt or perish. In 150 years of life the club has shown remarkable talents for survival, for seeking out and exploiting the competitive edge.

Today's problems, challenges, may often seem insurmountable. It has always been so; the hangnail of the moment is always more painful than last week's migraine. It is for that reason that the reading of history is salutory. At the moment of pain, a small voice of humility intrudes to say, "We have suffered before and survived."

It is this search for the competitive edge – the buoyant assertion to the right to survive – that unites the members of the club. Differences may divide them elsewhere, in their political affiliations, in their places of worship. But as members of the TCSCC they stand united. It is the strength of the members, the pride of the club, the pleasure of the game.

a

Abbiss, Mrs D.H.
A'Court, J.H.
Adam, J.S.
Adams, Andrew A.W.
Adams, Jeremy J.
Adams, Mrs R.H.
Adams, Robert W.
Adams, Mrs R.W.
Adams, Ronald G.
Adams, Miss Rosalind D.
Adams, Mrs W.H.A.
Adamson, W.G.
Adamson, Mrs W.G.
Adler, Dr W.V.
Adler, Mrs W.V.
Adomeit, Rolf
Aitchison, Mrs I.A.
Aitken, Graham C.
Aitken, Mrs G.C.
Albright, Miss Deborah L.
Albright, Gregor W.
Aldridge, Miss Deborah
Aldridge, Ronald C.
Alexander, Mrs R.G.H.
Allan, Chas. C.
Allan, Mrs C.C.
Allen, J.D.
Allen, Mrs J.D.
Allen, Mrs K.E.
Allen, T.J.
Allison, William A.
Alsop, Geo. T.
Alsop, Mrs G.T.
Ames, John W.
Ames, Kenner C.
Amey, Mrs Eleanor
Amey, Miss Stephanie
Ancuta, Mrs Shirley J.
Ander, Bruce
Ander, R.E.
Ander, Mrs R.E.
Anderson, Mrs A.H.
Anderson, Andrew S.
Anderson, Arthur W.
Anderson, David D.
Anderson, Derek H.
Anderson, Edward J.
Anderson, Mrs G.D.
Anderson, Gordon D.
Anderson, Jas. C.S.
Anderson, Mrs J.C.S.
Anderson, Mrs J.A.
Anderson, John N.
Anderson, Miss Laurie
Anderson, M.H.
Anderson, Mrs M.H.
Anderson, R.J.
Anderson, Mrs R.J.
Anderson, Robert J.
Anderson, Mrs Robt. J.

Anderson, Robert M.
Anderson, Mrs R.M.
Anderson, T.L.M.
Anderson, Miss Wendy E.
Andrew, Donald E.
Andrew, Mrs D.E.
Andrew, Edward D.
Andrus, David G.C.
Annett, Douglas R.
Archer, E.G.
Archibald, Chas. W.
Archibald, Mrs Lloyd
Archibald, Malcolm S.
Archibald, Mrs M.S.
Armitage, Blair F.
Armstrong, Edward C.
Armstrong, H.D.
Armstrong, Mrs H.D.
Armstrong, Peter W.
Armstrong, Mrs R.J.
Armstrong, Robert P.
Armstrong, Mrs R.P.
Arnoff, Miss Susan
Arnold, Dr Robin
Arnold, Mrs R.
Arnup, Harold L.
Arnup, Justice John D.
Arthur, John I.
Arthur, Mrs J.I.
Ash, Mrs C.L.
Ash, Miss Mary
Ashley, Cedric W.
Ashley, Mrs C.W.
Ashton, Miss Alison
Ashworth, Dr Murray A.
Ashworth, Mrs M.A.
Atwood, Ken. I.
Auger, Eliot M.
Austerberry, Mrs J.B.
Austerberry, Miss Shirlene H.
Austin, Arthur G.
Avery, Roy C.
Avery, Mrs R.C.
Axmith, Mrs M.E.
Aylesworth, Hon John B.

b

Babcock, Mrs H.A.
Babensee, John H.
Bailey, Karen L.
Bailey, Wm. K.
Bailey, Wm. J.L.
Bailey, Mrs W.J.L.
Bain, Geo. K.
Bain, Mrs Geo. K.
Baird, Mrs R.C.

Baker, Donald K.
Baker, Douglas G.
Baker, J.J.
Baker, Kenneth A.
Baker, Mrs K.A.
Baker, Thos. H.
Bale, Stephen T.
Ballentine, Mrs A.B.
Ballantyne, Ian A.
Ballantyne, Mrs I.A.
Ballantyne, Peter
Baltz, Ernest M.
Baltz, Mrs E.M.
Band, Miss Mary G.
Barber, Mrs W.R.
Barbour, Edward R.
Barnes, Chas. H.
Barton, Donald E.
Barton, Mrs D.E.
Barton, Mrs H.G.
Barrett, Leslie C.
Barrett, Mrs L.C.
Barrie, Miss Diane P.
Barrington, Mrs Mary
Bassingthwaighte, Mrs E.M.
Bastien, Richard W.
Bata, Thos. J.
Batterson, Jonathon E.
Bawden, Jas. J.
Beacom, Bruce A.
Beacom, Mrs B.A.
Beamish, Robin A.
Beard, Mrs M. Dudley
Bearg, Mrs Gerrie
Bearg, Mitchell D.
Bearg, Stephen
Beattie, Ann M.
Beattie, Fred A.
Beattie, Miss Jane L.
Beattie, Mrs R.G.
Beattie, Robert G.
Beattie, Robert W.
Beattie, Thos. F.
Beazer, Mrs W.
Beazer, Wayne D.
Bechert, Miss M.E.
Becker, Fred A.
Becker, Mrs F.A.
Becker, Robert
Bedolfe, Robert M.
Beechinor, Mrs J.J.
Beekman, Philip E.
Beeson, Richard C.
Belcher, Miss Irene
Bell, Mrs J. Renwick
Bell, Mrs R.G.
Bell, Richard
Belyea, Mrs Helen A.
Benjamin, Mrs Johanna
Benson, Craig H.
Benson, John E.
Benson, Miss Meredy
Bent, Mrs Vera C.
Bentley, Jas.
Bentley, Mrs J.
Bentley, Miss Janis M.
Bere, Mrs Donns

161

Berry, L.M.
Berry, Peter C.
Bertram, R.C.
Bethune, Mrs N.W.
Bethune, Mrs Norman
Bethune, Miss Susan
Bethune, Miss Wendy
Betts, Miss Mary Lynn
Beverley, Mrs A.R.
Bezic, Dusan
Bezic, Miss Sandra M.
Bezic, Val
Bicknell, Mrs A.B.
Bigelow, Dr J.A.
Bigelow, Mrs J.A.
Bigelow, Robert H.
Bigelow, Mrs R.H.
Biggs, Dr M.
Biggs, Mrs M.
Biggs, Jeffrey I.P.
Biggs, Richard C.
Billinghurst, Miss Geral
Billinghurst, P.W.
Billinghurst, Mrs P.W.
Billingsley, Mrs Robt.
Binnie, Robert W.H.
Binnie, Mrs R.W.H.
Binnie, J. Scott M.
Bird, Richard R.
Blaber, Mrs H.B.
Blaber, Hugh B.
Black, Mrs Eric J.
Black, Robin C.
Black, Mrs M.S.
Blain, Miss Elizabeth A.
Blair, Mrs Christina
Blair, Miss Cindy Lee
Blair, Miss Marilyn G.
Blair, Ross A.
Blair, Mrs R.A.
Blair, Stephen R.
Blakely, Robt. W.
Blanchflower, Colin A.
Blanchflower, Mrs C.
Blink, Gino
Blink, Mrs G.
Blyth, W.D.
Blyth, Mrs W.D.
Boadway, C.W.
Boadway, Mrs C.W.
Boake, Kingdom B.
Bodley, J. Douglas
Bodley, Mrs J.D.
Body, David
Boire, Geo. A.
Boire, Mrs G.A.
Boire, Roger E.
Boland, Mrs C.
Bolton, Carmen J.
Bolton, Mrs Ron
Bone, Bruce C.
Bone, Mrs B.C.
Bone, Brian C.
Bone, Peter W.
Bone, Ronald K.
Bonus, W.H.
Booker, Reg. J.

Booker, Mrs R.J.
Booth, Mrs J.K.B.
Boothroyd, Mrs Dorothy
Borczon, Walter H.
Borczon, Mrs W.H.
Boskill, P.A.
Boskill, Mrs P.A.
Bourdon, Harvey A.
Bourdon, Mrs H.A.
Bourne, Les. A.
Bovaird, J.B.
Bovaird, Mrs J.B.
Bovaird, Timothy
Bowden, Mrs J.A.
Bowden, Miss Judith A.
Bowden, Norris
Bowerman, Miss Julie A.
Bowes, James C.
Bowes, Mrs J.C.
Bowlby, Bradford H.B.
Bowlby, Miss Anne E.
Bowness, Dr E.R.
Box, Dr Thos. R.H.
Box, Miss Kathryn
Boyle, W. Harold
Brace, W.M.
Brace, Mrs W.M.
Bracht, E.A.
Bracht, Norman
Bradbury, Mrs W.J.
Bradford, Mrs D.E.
Bradford, Mrs Frances
Bradley, Chas. J.
Bradley, Mrs C.J.
Bradley, Miss Megan L.
Bradley, Miss Paula A.
Bradley, Michael G.
Brankovsky, Miss Barbara
Brannan, C.E.
Branscombe, Dr E.S.
Branscombe, Mrs E.S.
Branscombe, Miss Robin M.
Brebner, D.A.
Brebner, Mrs D.A.
Brennan, Mrs D.C.
Brett, Douglas
Breithaupt, Mrs P.W.
Breithaupt, Miss M.J.
Brethour, Riley N.
Brethour, Miss Elizabeth
Brethour, Miss Margaret
Brodie, Lt Col Le Sueur
Brodeur, P.L.
Brooker, Mrs D.J.
Brooker, Miss Deborah M.
Brooker, Ian
Brooks, Mrs C.D.
Brooks, Murray N.
Brown, Denis W.
Brown, Dennis W.
Brown, Mrs Dorothy
Brown, Iain G.L.
Brown, Miss K.E.
Brown, L.B.
Brown, Mrs L.B.
Brown, Miss Linda C.E.
Brown, Miss Marilyn

Brown, Robert M.
Brown, Thomas
Brown, T.C.
Brown, Mrs T.C.
Brown, Mrs T.F.S.
Brunt, Mrs W.R.
Bryce, Mrs Lillian M.
Bryce, Peter
Bryce, Mrs P.
Buchan, J.M.
Buchan, J.N.
Buchanan, H.G.
Buck, H.D.R.
Buck, Mrs H.D.R.
Buck, Miss Laura E.
Buckingham, Brian
Buckley, Frank C.
Buckley, Mrs F.C.
Buffam, Mrs B.S.W.
Buik, Mrs W.A.
Bull, John G.S.
Bull, Mrs J.S.
Buller, John R.
Buntic, Miss Anne
Burka, Miss Petra
Burn, Peter F.H.
Burnham, Mrs H.H.
Burgess, A. James
Burnside, W.G.
Burridge, Miss Claire E.
Burrows, Ron G.
Burrows, Mrs Patricia
Burrows, Mrs W.H.R.
Burson, Miss Esther M.
Burson, Herbert R.
Burson, George E.
Burton, Mrs M.W.
Butler, Barry T.
Bythell, Donald C.
Bythell, Mrs D.C.

Cadogan, Dr George I.
Cadogan, Mrs G.I.
Cairns, Dr J.D.
Caldwell, Clive T.
Caldwell, Mrs C.T.
Caldwell, H.B.
Caldwell, Mrs H.B.
Campbell, David A.
Campbell, Miss Jane E.
Campbell, Miss Jessie
Campbell, Dr Stanley M.
Campbell, Mrs S.M.
Cane, Chas. H.W.
Cannon, Mrs D.B.
Capeling, Mrs Greta S.
Cappon, Dr D.
Carley, Alex J.

Carlyle, D.B.
Carmichael, Allan
Carscallen, Ernest N.
Carscallen, Mrs E.N.
Carscallen, Miss Merry K.
Carscallen, Miss Susan C.
Carson, A.M.
Carter, Mrs C.F.
Carton, Mrs Gordon
Carver, Ross D.
Carveth, Arthur H.
Carveth, Gordon H.
Carveth, Mrs G.H.
Carruthers, Clare D.
Carruthers, Mrs C.D.
Cassels, Chas. L.
Cassels, Leith M.
Cassels, Stewart G.
Cassels, Mrs S.G.
Casson, Dr Ian R.
Casson, Peter
Casson, Richard
Caswell, Ralph S.
Catto, Chas. E.
Cauley, John S.
Cauley, Mrs J.S.
Caulfield, Miss P. Ann
Caulfied, Ronald A.
Cayley, Alasdair C.S.
Cayley, Miss Briony J.
Cayley, F.W.
Cernik, Chas.
Cernik, John R.
Cernik, Mrs J.R.
Chalmers, Dr J.L.
Chalmers, Mrs J.L.
Chambers, Fred
Chambers, Mrs F.
Chambers, Harold J.A.
Chambers, Dr H.R.
Chambers, Mrs H.R.
Chaplin, Dr Robt. A.
Chapman, Albert N.
Chapman, Mrs A.N.
Chapman, Barry M.
Chapman, Mrs B.M.
Chapman, Miss Beverley
Chapman, Bradley J.
Chapman, Mrs B.J.
Chapman, Robert J.
Chapman, Mrs R.J.
Chapman, Mrs W.R.
Chappell, Chris. J.D.
Charron, Dr R.
Cheesbrough, Gordon F.
Cherry, Alan J.
Cherry, Mrs A.J.
Cheskin, Mrs Margaret M.F.
Cholette, Robert D.
Cholette, Mrs R.D.
Chown, Mrs E.B.
Church, Kenneth E.
Cimetta, Angelo
Cimetta, Mrs A.
Clark, Allan J.
Clark, Mrs A.J.
Clark, Mrs Florence M.

Clark, Mrs J.R.
Clark, Miss Mary E.
Clark, Norman C.O.
Clark, Mrs N.C.O.
Clark, Dr R.K.
Clark, Wm. B.
Clark, Mrs W.B.
Clarke, Mrs A.
Clarke, Donald Gordon
Clarke, H.A.
Clarke, Mrs H.A.
Clarke, D.P.
Clarke, Mrs D.P.
Clarke, F.B.
Clarke, Mrs F.B.
Clarke, Mrs G.C.
Clarke, Mrs J.L.
Clarke, John
Clarke, Dr K.S.
Clarke, Mrs K.S.
Clarke, Miss Susan D.
Cleather, E.G.
Cleworth, Miss Victoria A.
Clifford, Robert M.
Cline, Fred M.
Clippindale, John L.M.
Clow, Stuart E.
Clow, Mrs S.E.
Cocks, Miss Carolyn S.
Code, Miss Muriel A.
Cole, Dr Arthur R.C.
Coles, Hume A.
Coles, Mrs H.A.
Colquhoun, Ian A.
Colson, H.O.
Coman, Alan C.
Comer, Mrs J.F.
Conacher, Mrs Lionel
Conde, Michael H.
Conde, Mrs M.H.
Conner, G.M.
Cooke, Mrs K.
Coombs, Mrs M.J.
Cooper, Wilfred J.
Copeland, Wm. C.
Corkill, Dr J.M.B.
Corneil, Bruce L.
Cornell, Clarence E.
Cornwell, John
Cornwell, Reg. B.
Corpes, John L.
Cossitt, Edwin
Cotnam, Harvey A.
Coughlin, Debra A.
Coughlin, Victor L.
Coughlin, Mrs V.L.
Coulter, Mrs R.J.G.
Coultis, Douglas
Coultis, Mrs D.G.
Court, Jas. D.
Coutts, Douglas R.
Coutts, Mrs Mary Ellen
Coutts, James E.
Cowan, Richard J.
Cowie, Mrs Alfred H.
Cowl, George
Cowl, Mrs G.

Cowles, Mrs J.N.B.
Cowley, Mrs Leigh
Craig, John A.D.
Cramer, Mrs A.H.
Cranston, Toller M.
Crawford, Bradley
Crawford, Mrs B.
Crawford, Dr Reeve
Crawford, Wm. E.
Crawford, Mrs W.E.
Creasy, Mrs D.E.J.
Creswicke, Miss Edith
Crocker, Bunting S.
Croil, Thos. A.
Crossey, Richard E.
Crossey, Mrs R.E.
Crossley, Anthony K.H.
Crossley, Kenneth J.H.
Crossley, Mrs K.J.H.
Cruikshank, Mrs Aidrie
Cruikshank, Miss Elizabeth
Cruikshank, Michael B.
Cruikshank, Mrs M.B.
Crummer, R.W.
Crysdale, Mrs P.S.
Cuff, Dr Thos. W.
Cullens, Wm. S.
Cumming, Mrs N.
Cunningham, Miss Leslie J.
Cunnington, Mrs M.E.
Currie, Ian W.
Cutbush, Douglas F.
Cutler, Miss J.K.

Dabolczi-Fekete, Miss Dominique
Dafoe, Mrs Helen G.
Dafoe, John E.
Dafoe, Wm. A.
Dafoe, Mrs W.A.
d'Agincourt, Harvey
Dake, Mrs Naomi L.
Dalby, Mrs Rita
Dale, Mrs H.J.
Dalton, Mrs P.D.
Dalziel, Mrs D.K.
Dalziel, Robert I.
Dalziel, Wm. B.
Daniel, C.E.
Daniel, Mrs C.E.
Darling, W.W.G.
Davidson, Thos. G.M.
Davidson, Robert
Davis, Mrs H.A.
Davis, Kent J.

Davison, Louis M.
Davison, Mrs L.M.
Davison, Mrs J.A.
Dawson, Mrs J.R.
Day, Chas. W.R.
Daykin, H.A.
Dean, Alan W.
Dean, Mrs A.W.
Dean, Brian G.
Dean, Miss M.A.
Dean, Peter
Dean, Stuart C.
Dean, Mrs S.C.
Dean, Stuart C. Jr.
Decker, Chris. J.
Decker, John
Dee, Richard B.
Degeer, Garry E.
deGuerre, Warren H.
deGuerre, Mrs W.H.
Delamere, Mrs H.D.
Del Zotto, Leo. D.
Del Zotto, Mrs L.D.
Dempster, Robt. N.
Dennis, Miss Elizabeth J.T.
Dennis, Peter A.
Deratnay, Edward C.
Deratnay, Mrs E.C.
Deratnay, George G.
Deratnay, Mrs G.G.
De Soto, Mrs E.
De Soto, Juan
Devlin, James J.
Devlin, Tim. B.
Dewar, Miss Margaret E.
De Weerdt, F.M.
Dick, John G.
Dick, Mrs J.G.
Dick, Miss Judith
Dick, Mrs W.J.
Dickie, George H.
Dickinson, John
Dickinson, Mrs J.
Dillon, Mrs Thos. A.
Dimock, Mrs F.C.
Dinkla, Emil
Dinkla, Mrs E.
Dinkla, Ralph
Dinsmore, Mrs K.M.
Dixon, Ross
Dobson, R.C.
Dodge, Andrew A.
Dodge, Mrs A.A.
Doggett, Geo. F.
Doherty, A.M.
Doherty, Mrs A.M.
Doherty, Mrs B.
Doherty, Franklin J.
Dolan, James P.
Domelle, J.H.
Domm, Earl C.
Donohue, Dr Wm. L.
Doran, Jas. K.
Douglas, Angus
Douglas, Clifford L.
Douglas, Mrs C.L.
Douglas, Stuart M.

Douglas, Miss Virginia L.
Dover, Mrs C.F.
Dover, Miss Nancy
Dowding, John S.
Downey, Bruce C.
Downey, Mrs B.C.
Drawbell, Donald M.
Dryden, John R.
Duckworth, A. Gordon
Duff, Graeme R.
Duff, J.R.
Duff, Mrs J.R.
Duff, Miss Margaret E.
Duff, Prescott T.
Dumas, Mrs W.M.
Duncan, J. Rod.
Duncan, Mrs J.R.
Dunlop, David W.S.
Dunlop, Ronald W.
Dunsmore, R.L.
Dunton, Mrs F.W.
Dussault, Miss Diane
Dussault, Jean J.
Dussault, Mrs J.J.
Dussault, Miss Nicole
Dye, Mrs S.E.
Dyer, Joseph W.
Dymott, Anthony A.
Dymott, Mrs A.A.

e

Eagan, Richard V.P.
Early, Mrs Mary
Eastwood, Jack C.
Eaton, George R.
Ebert, Mrs H.J.
Edgar, Mrs Todd
Edmund, Miss Linda J.
Edwards, Eric H.
Edwards, Mrs E.H.
Edwards, Miss Ericka P.
Egerdie, Mrs Anne
Egerdie, Blair
Egerdie, Grant
Egerdie, Russell F.
Ekmekjian, David M.
Ekmekjian, Mrs D.M.
el Baroudi, Dr M.Y.
Elder, John J.
Elliott, Mrs J. Peter
Elliott, Norman J.
Elliott, Mrs N.J.
Elmsley, J.B.
Elsley, Mrs. W.B.
Emmett, Dr J.A.J.
Emmett, Mrs J.A.J.
Enns, George R.
Enns, Mrs G.R.
Esson, Ian D.W.
Etherington, Nigel
Evans, Miss Elizabeth J.

Evans, Eric
Evans, Mrs Marjorie J.
Evenson, Lloyd R.
Evenson, Mrs L.R.
Evenson, Miss Jane E.
Evenson, Jeffrey D.
Evenson, Richard
Everitt, W.E.

Fahlenbock, Terrence D.
Fahlenbock, Mrs T.D.
Fahlgren, Mrs D.G.
Fahlgren, Miss Kathleen M.
Fahlgren, Terry E.
Fanning, Robt. F.
Farrell, Hugh R.
Farrell, Roderick H.
Farwell, Alfred W.G.
Farwell, Mrs A.W.G.
Fawcett, Donald F.
Felesko, Randle S.C.
Felesko, Roger
Felesko, Mrs R.
Fenn, Anthony N.
Fenn, Mrs A.N.
Fenn, Giles P.
Fenn, Ronald A.
Fenton, Mrs C.R.
Fenwick, Ronald H.W.
Ferguson, Mrs B.R.
Ferguson, Donald S.
Ferguson, Gerald A.
Ferguson, Gordon R.
Ferguson, R. Norman
Ferguson, Mrs R.N.
Ferguson, Wm. J.
Fiedler, Mrs A.W.
Filkin, Mrs C.E.
Fillo, M.F.
Fillo, Mrs M.F.
Finlayson, Donald C.
Finlayson, Mrs D.C.
Finlayson, Douglas C.
Finlayson, Miss Shiona E.
Fisher, Mrs Catherine A.
Fisher, Mrs E.M.S.
Fleming, Arnold
Fleming, David W.
Fleming, Mrs D.W.
Fleming, Hon Donald M.
Fleming, Heather Lynn
Fleming, Mrs John P.
Fleming, Richard A.
Fleming, Dr Wm. A.E.
Fleming, Mrs W.A.E.
Fleming-Wood, David J.A.

Fleming-Wood, Mrs D.J.A.
Flett, John F.
Flett, Mrs J.F.
Flowers, John W.
Flowers, Mrs J.W.
Floyd, Roger J.
Floyd, Mrs R.J.
Flynn, Miss Diana L.
Foley, Howard Dale
Foley, Mrs K.A.
Forbes, Donald
Forbes, Miss Joan S.
Forbes, Miss Karen L.
Ford, G. Robert
Foster, Mrs Andrew A.
Foster, C.W.D.
Foster, Mrs J.R.
Foster, John Robert
Foster, Robert H.
Foulds, Kenneth A.
Frampton, Arthur H.
Francis, Wm. F.
Francis, Mrs W.F.
Fraser, D. Ian
Fraser, Mrs D.I.
Fraser, Miss Heather M.
Fraser, John G.
Fraser, Mrs J.R.
Fraser, Norman G.
Fraser, Mrs N.G.
Fraser, Mrs R.A.
Fraser, Mrs R.S.
Fraser, T.O.
Frederick, Dolliver H.
Frederick, John C.
French, Derek
French, Robert T.
Frewer, John D.
Fricker, Eric
Friesen, Douglas L.
Frost, Miss Donna E.
Frost, W.A.E.
Frost, Mrs W.A.E.
Furlong, Dr F.W.
Furlong, Mrs F.W.
Furse, Mrs Hazel
Fyvie, Mrs Douglas

g

Gagley, Miss Rita M.
Gale, Chief Justice G.A.
Gale, Mrs G.A.
Galipeault, Andre
Galipeault, Mrs A.J.
Galloway, James E.
Galloway, Murray G.
Galloway, Mrs M.G.

Garden, Miss Janet E.
Gardhouse, Mrs Charline J.
Gardhouse, Judge Geo. W.
Gardiner, Ralph
Garriock, Mrs R.G.
Geddes, Miss Agatha
Geleziunas, Joseph
Geleziunas, Mrs J.
Geller, Mrs H.
Geoghegan, Mrs J.M.
George, Mrs A.F.
Gerrard, Alan
Gerred, Dr Ralph F.
Gerred, Ralph K.
Gershater, Dr Raziel
Gershater, Mrs R.
Gerstl, Miss Sherry R.
Gibson, Campbell B.
Gibson, Clarence
Gibson, David C.
Gibson, Elbert E.
Gibson, Ian M.
Giffen, Mrs Jas. P.
Gilchrist, Donald H.
Gill, James M.
Gill, Mrs J.M.
Gillespie, J.B.
Gillespie, Mrs J.B.
Gillespie, John D.H.
Gillies, Miss Kimberly
Gillham, Miss Susan
Gillies, Arnold E.
Glass, Mrs Cecilia L.
Glasscock, Mrs G.H.
Glover, Henry S.
Glover, Mrs H.S.
Godson, Robert G.
Goldring, Thos. F.
Goldring, Mrs T.F.
Goldsmith, John J.R.
Goldsmith, Mrs J.J.
Goldsmith, Miss Mary F.
Gooderham, Mrs E.D.
Goodman, Mrs Jean R.
Goodman, Dr Wilfred S.
Goodman, Mrs W.S.
Goodwin, John G.
Gordon, David E.
Gordon, John C.L.
Gordon, Mrs M.M.
Gorham, Mrs Mary T.
Gorman, M.F.J.
Gornall, Dr Allan
Gornall, Mrs A.G.
Gorrie, Frederick R.
Gorrie, Mrs F.R.
Gossage, Dr John D.
Gossage, Mrs J.D.
Gough, Mrs Barbara
Gouinlock, Robert W.
Gouinlock, Mrs R.W.
Gourlay, Miss A.
Gouveia, Keith A.
Gower, Miss Kathleen
Graham, Mrs Audrey E.
Graham, Chas. W.
Graham, Clarence W.

Graham, Miss Glenna
Graham, Dr John E.
Graham, Mrs J.E.
Graham, Dr Michael R.
Graham, Mrs M.R.
Graham, Wm. T.
Grange, E. Rochfort
Grant, Miss A.E.
Grant, Mrs Catherine A.
Grant, Dana W.
Grant, Mrs D.W.
Grant, George M.
Grant, Mrs G.M.
Grant, Miss Gwynneth R.
Grant, Miss Jane C.
Grant, Miss Janet E.
Grant, Terence P.
Grant, Mrs T.P.
Grant, William A.
Gray, Mrs Ann
Gray, Mrs Clifford J.
Gray, Goerge M.
Gray, Mrs G.M.
Gray, James G.
Gray, Kenneth J.
Gray, Michael E.
Gray, Peter C.
Green, Harold
Green, Mrs H.
Green, Kevin
Green, M.S.
Green, Mrs M.S.
Green, Michael A.S.
Greenfield, Mrs A. Jean
Greenshields, John
Grieco, Miss Ginnie L.
Grieve, Mrs Hugh
Grieve, Mrs J.A.
Grieve, John N.
Grieve, Mrs J.N.
Griffen, Barry E.
Grimshaw, Miss D. Margaret
Grimshaw, Dr Isobel
Grogan, Mrs Barbara
Grover, John K.M.
Guest, Mrs David G.
Gundy, Jas. H.C.
Gunn, Chas. A.
Gunn, Nigel H.
Gunn, Mrs N.H.
Guoba, Mrs J.
Guthrie, Albert

h

Habib, Miss Christine D.
Habib, Jerry H.

165

Habib, Mrs Laurice
Hadden, John
Hakes, Dr John A.A.
Haley, Miss Donna J.
Hall, Mrs Anne C.
Hall, Basil T. Jr.
Hall, Donald G.
Hall, Mrs Donald G.
Hall, James A.
Hall, Philip
Halliwell, Miss Patricia
Halmay, Steve
Halsall, Miss Rita
Hamer, Alexander
Hamer, Mrs Dorothy
Hamer, John E.
Hamill, Miss Dorothy
Hamilton, Mrs J.
Hamilton, John J.
Hamilton, Mrs M.B.
Hamilton, Ross T.
Hamilton, Sidney B.
Hamilton, Wm. E.
Hampton, Miss Laura
Hansen, Mrs Andrea
Hardman, Walter E.
Hare, Edward F.
Hargraft, Miss Helen G.
Harling, Miss Carol A.
Harling, R. Donald
Harling, Mrs R.D.
Harling, Mrs R.S.
Harling, Thos. D.
Harling, Mrs T.D.
Harling, Thos. R.
Harling, Mrs T.R.
Harlock, Kenneth L.
Harlock, Mrs K.L.
Harris, Guy L.
Harris, Mrs G.L.
Harris, Mrs J.W.
Harris, Dr L.D.
Harris, Scott L.
Harper, Alfred E.
Harper, Mrs A.E.
Hart, Miss Deborah L.
Hartman, Mrs L.
Harvey, John C.
Harvey, Mrs J.C.
Harvey, Thos. E.
Haskell, Miss Marion
Hasler, John
Hatton, Michael J.
Hawken, Mrs E.F.
Hawryliw, Wm. V.
Hay, Miss E.M.
Hayes, Alastair B.
Hayman, Robert C.
Hayter, Harold W.
Hayward, John
Haywood, Mrs K.D.
Hazlett, D.
Healy, Mrs J.B.
Heard, Roderick G.
Hearn, John R.
Hearn, Mrs J.R.
Heath, Beverley

Heaton, Mrs T.G.
Heaton, Miss Catherine M.
Hebb, Laurence D.
Hedstrom, Mrs Cecil
Heffelfinger, Mrs L.E.
Heighington, Robt.
Heiland, Miss Donna M.
Heiland, Michael
Heiland, Patrick A.
Heiland, Philip A.
Heiland, Mrs P.A.
Heilmann, Ross
Heintzman, Mrs George C.
Heller, Mrs Alice
Heller, Henry P.
Heller, Mrs Rosaleen
Helwig, Carl E.
Hemmant, Miss Janet C.
Hemmant, John P.
Hemmant, Mrs J.P.
Hemmant, Miss N. Joanne
Henderson, Arthur C.
Henderson, Mrs A.C.
Henderson, Miss Elizabeth
Hendry, Edward A.
Henry, Miss Sally
Henwood, Mrs Susan
Hepburn, Harold L.
Hepburn, Mrs H.L.
Hermant, Adam B.T.
Hermant, Sydney
Hermant, Mrs S.
Hervey, Eugene H.
Hewett, F. Robert
Hewitt, Jas. A.
Hewitt, Mrs J.A.
Hewitt, Robert
Hewitt, Mrs R.
Heymans, Donald
Heymans, Mrs D.
Hibben, Alan R.
Hicks-Lyne, Mrs R.T.E.
Higgerson, John F.
Hildebrand, Edward C.
Hill, Clarke R.
Hill, Donald D.
Hill, Mrs D.D.
Hill, Mrs F.W.
Hill, Mrs E.M.
Hill, Mrs L.M.
Hill, J. Rowland
Hill, Miss Patricia L.
Hill, Miss Rebecca H.
Hill, W. Fred
Hille, Miss Monica-Anne
Hiscox, Miss Catherine A.
Hisey, Dennis
Hisey, Steven
Hisey, Mrs S.
Hisey, Miss Virginia
Histrop, Miss Lindsay A.
Hoare, Dr D.S.
Hoare, Mrs D.S.
Hochberg, Ian D.
Hochberg, Joseph
Hodges, J.R.
Hodgart, Dr Alice E.

Hogg, Frank F.
Hogg, Thos.
Holden, Waldo J.
Holland, D.A.
Holley, Mrs J.S.
Holmes, Campbell C.
Holmes, Mrs C.C.
Holmes, David C.
Holmes, Miss P. Virginia
Holmes, T.A.
Home, Wallace G.
Holtby, Mrs Beulah M.
Holwell, H.N.
Holwell, Miss Nikki
Hood, Miss Jane E.
Hood, Mrs W.D.
Hooey, Wayne L.
Hooey, Mrs W.L.
Hoogstraten, Jacques J.A.
Hoogstraten, Miss M.G.L.M.
Hooper, John S.
Hooper, Mrs J.S.
Hord, Mrs A.B.
Horsman, Gordon L.
Houston, Donald M.
Houston, Robert S.
Howard, Mrs A.L.
Howard, David E.
Howard, Mrs D.E.
Howe, Mrs S.M.
Howson, Miss Jean
Hubbell, John R.
Huckle, Jack W.
Huckle, Mrs J.W.
Hudakoc, Mrs Heather P.
Hudakoc, John R.P.
Hughes, Richard N.
Hughes, Samuel G.S.
Hull, Frank F.
Hull, Mrs F.F.
Hume, William C.
Hume, Mrs W.C.
Humphry, Jas.
Humphries, Wm. B.G.
Hunt, Jas. C.
Hunt, Mrs J.E.
Hunter, George A.A.
Hunter, Lorne M.
Hunter, Richard F.
Hunter, Mrs R.F.
Hutchinson, Mrs J.R.
Hyatt, E.J.
Hyatt, Mrs E.J.
Hyde, Alexander G.
Hyland, J. Gordon
Hynes, Miss Sally R.

Iggulden, Paul G.
Imeson, Mrs Susan

Innes, James C.
Innes, Richard D.
Innes, Mrs R.D.
Inksater, Jas. R.
Ireland, John
Ireton, Miss Elizabeth
Irvine, W.M.
Irvine, Mrs W.M.
Irvine, Walter M.
Irving, Thos. G.
Irwin, Miss Cathy L.
Irwin, Fred P.
Irwin, F.M. Jr.
Irwin, Mrs Karl
Irwin, Peter M.
Ivey, D.G.
Ivey, Mrs D.G.
Ivey, Miss Sharon E.
Ivic, Leopold
Iwanyk, Walter

j

Jackson, Geoffrey J.
Jackson, Harry
Jackson, Mrs H.
Jackson, Leonard
Jacob, Robert
Jacob, Mrs R.P.
Jacobs, Dr Wm. F.
Jaeger, H. Heinz
James, Chas. C.
James, Mrs C.C.
James, David M.
James, Michael R.
Jamieson, John H.
Janiss, Dr Eugene
Jarrell, Mrs W.A.
Jarrott, Jack H.
Jarvis, Mrs A.E.
Jasperson, Mrs F.B.
Jeffrey, Frank M.
Jemmett, John L.
Jemmett, Philip A.
Jenkins, D.G.
Jenkins, Lock S.
Jensen, Harald
Jensen, Mrs H.
Jenset, Anton
Jenset, Mrs A.
Jenset, John M.
Jewell, Paul Ross, QC
Jewell, Mrs P.R.

Johns, Arthur E.
Johns, Janet L.
Johnson, Denis C.
Johnson, Mrs D.C.
Johnson, Mrs J.B.
Johnson, Michael B.J.
Johnston, Albert McK.
Johnston, Mrs A.M.
Johnston, Miss Barbara M.
Johnston, Miss Beverly J.
Johnston, Jas. G.
Johnston, Mrs J.G.
Johnston, Wm. E.
Johnstone, Mrs Gregory
Jones, Miss Barbara
Jones, Mrs Beatrice
Jones, Miss Gwyneth A.
Jones, Leslie T.
Jones, Mrs O.T.C.
Jones, Dr R.B.
Jones, Mrs W.A.M.
Jory, M.D.
Josephs, Miss Judi
Josephs, Leon J.
Joyce, John T.
Joyce, Mrs J.T.
Joyce, Wm. K.
Jurczynski, Andrew R.

k

Kane, Miss Cynthia M.
Kane, Mrs J.C.
Kane, Lawrence A.
Kane, R.J.
Kane, Thos. D.
Kasta, Brian C.
Kasta, Mrs B.C.
Katz, Dr Allan
Katz, Mrs A.
Keachie, Jas. B.
Keachie, Mrs J.B.
Keeler, Ronald H.
Kellam, Frank W.
Kellam, Reg. H.
Kelly, Dr D.A.
Kelly, Mrs D.A.
Kelly, Leonard P.
Kelly, Mrs L.P.
Kelton, Mrs Robert C.
Kemkaran, Dr Samuel K.
Kemp, Frederick W.

Kennard, David W.
Kennedy, Frank A.
Kennedy, Dr John E.
Kennedy, Wm. D.
Kenner, Mrs H.B.
Kenny, Miss Margaret
Kerruish, Mrs H.B.
Keshavji, Moshin
Keslick, Robt. J.
Kester, Mrs A.R.
Kettle, Horace G.
Keys, Mrs Mary
Kidd, Miss Bessie E.
Kiely, Mrs Mark
Kilpatrick, George B.
Kimball, Mrs R.H.
King, Mrs C.C.
King, Mrs Thos.
Kinnear, John C.
Kinnear, Mrs J.C.
Kinsey, Peter T.
Kirk, Chas. B.
Kirkland, Robt. W.
Kirkpatrick, A.W.M.
Kirkpatrick, Arch. M.
Kirkpatrick, Mrs H.V.
Knapp, Robt. J.
Knox, Ralph D.
Knox, Mrs R.D.
Koehler, Rudy A.
Koruna, Robert W.
Koster, Mrs Carolyn
Kostiw, Walter
Kostiw, Mrs W.
Koyl, Dr Leon F.
Kramer, Mrs Helen
Krausz, George
Kristenbrun, Thos.
Kuttis, Nicholas

l

Labrie, John P.
Laceby, Geo. E.
Laframboise, Glenn T.
Laing, Mrs R.W.
Lamantia, Miss Michelina
Lane, Fred E.
Lane, Mrs F.E.
Lang, Mrs Harriet E.
Lang, Miss June D.M.
Lang, Miss Patricia L.H.
Langdon, Edwin S.
Langdon, Mrs E.S.

Langdon, Henry D.
Lanskail, Dr J.C.
Lanskail, Mrs J.C.
Lanskail, Miss Mary C.
Lantz, Floyd C.
Lantz, Mrs F.C.
Large, Mrs F.T.
Lascelles, Geoffrey A.
Lascelles, John A.
Latimer, John R.
Laverock, George D.
Law, Mrs S.G.
Lawrence, Miss Heather A.
Lawson, Hugh R.
Lawson, Mrs M.E.
Layton, Miss E.
Learmouth, Wm. R.
Leask, Miss Welda
Leckie, Gerald I.
Leckie, Mrs G.I.
Lederer, Derek J.M.
Lederer, Miss Jennifer M.
Lederer, Robert F.
Ledner, Mrs Heather
Lee, Ernest M.
Lee, Mrs E.M.
Legate, B.E.
Legate, Mrs B.E.
Legge, Mrs Chris. B.
Le Heup, Jon N.A.
LeMarquand, George H.
LeMarquand, Mrs G.H.
Lerner, Mrs Heather
Lewis, Walter David G.
Lewis, Mrs W.D.G.
Lewis, Wm. E.
Li, Daniel
Li, Mrs D.
Lickley, Dr H. Lavina
Lickley, J.T.F.
Liebman, Mrs Cynthia
Lillyman, Roger G.
Lillyman, Mrs R.G.
Lindner, Miss Margo E.
Linnell, Anthony J.
Linney, Donald R.
Linney, Mrs D.R.
Linney, Miss Patricia A.
Lipson, Dr Frank
Lipson, Mrs F.
Little, Dr Jas. A.
Little, Mrs J.A.
Little, Reg. A.
Little, Mrs R.A.
Littlejohn, R.H.
Litvinchuk, Miss Catherine A.
Litvinchuk, Mrs Olga
Livingstone, Blair A.
Livingstone, Mrs B.A.
Lloyd, Warren G.
Lloyd, Mrs W.G.
Loach, Alfred G.
Loach, Mrs A.G.
Lockhart, Mrs H.E.
Lofquist, Mrs John J.
Loman, Jack
Lombard, Mrs C.F.

Lombard, Miss Mary Jane
Lombard, Miss Susan J.
Lombard, Stuart C.
Lone, Mrs Elizabeth
Loney, E.F.
Loney, Miss Gioja M.
Long, Alfred J.M.
Long, Edward A.
Longstaffe, Mrs Nancy
Loriaux, Miss Louise
Lount, Mrs Harold F.
Love, Robert H.
Loveless, Robert I.
Lowes, A. West
Lowes, Barry G.
Lowes, Mrs B.G.
Lowes, Brit
Lowes, Judith E.
Lowes, Miss Kim
Lowidt, Miss Barbara H.
Lowidt, Mrs F.D.
Lowndes, Roy H.M.
Lucas, Gordon T.
Lucas, Mrs G.T.
Ludvik, Mrs Daniella
Luke, Dr Wm. R.F.
Lutton, Thos. G.
Lutton, Mrs T.G.
Lutton, Timothy C.
Lyall, Ed. M.
Lynch, John W.
Lynch, Scott W.
Lynch, W.D.
Lynch, Walker J.

m

Mabee, Mrs R.R.
MacBeth, Mrs J.P.
MacBeth, Miss Wendy J.
MacDiarmid, K.H., QC
MacDiarmid, Mrs K.H.
MacDonald, David J.
MacDonald, Dennis G.
MacDonald, Donald S.
MacDonald, Mrs J.K.
MacDonald, J.T.
MacDonald, Mrs Jody
MacDonald, John R.
Macdonald, Mrs D.C.
Macdonald, Dale A.
Macdonald, Douglas B.
Macdonald, Donald R.
MacDonell, Mrs John G.
MacDonell, Miss Sheila
MacDonell, Wm. D.

MacDonnell, Richard B.
MacEachern, Ian A.
MacEachern, Mrs I.A.
MacEachern, Ian B.
MacEachern, Norman A.
MacEwen, P.B.
MacEwen, Mrs P.B.
Macey, Mrs Gordon
MacGirr, Chas G.
MacGregor, Ian K.
Mach, Bernard
MacIver, Mrs Judith
Mackay, Alex. L.
Macken, Brenden H.
MacKenzie, Dr Ross G.
MacKenzie, Mrs R.G.
MacKenzie, Dr R.B.
Mackie, James M.
Mackie, Mrs J.M.
MacKillop, Mrs Patricia
MacKinnon, Peter
Macklin, Harold L.
Macklin, Mrs H.L.
MacLean, Alexander
MacLean, Mrs A.
MacLean, Douglas
MacLean, Gordon
MacLean, John D.
MacLean, Mrs J.D.
MacLean, John R.
MacLean, Harry C.
MacLean, I. Ross
MacLean, Jas. H.
MacLean, Mrs J.H.
MacNaughton, Mrs S.S.
MacNicol, Hugh
MacNicol, Mrs H.A.
MacNicol, Murray B.
MacPhail, Duncan T.
MacPherson, Miss Mary E.
MacTavish, L.R.
Madden, Andrew
Madden, Jeffrey
Madden, Mrs J.
Maddock, Miss Beverley J.
Maddock, Holmes R. III
Maddock, Mrs H.R.
Madill, Mrs Ruth
Magee, Miss Gayle J.
Magee, Harold W.
Magnus, Mrs Anke
Mahabir, Dr R.J.
Mahabir, Mrs R.J.
Mahoney, Jos. E.
Malcolmson, Mrs J.C.
Maltin, Mrs R.K.
Mann, Donald
Mann, Mrs D.C.
Mansfield, Miss Deborah J.
Manzie, Gordon
Margesson, Mrs Maurice P.
Margison, John E.
Mariani, Daniel
Mariani, Erick
Marks, Giles D.
Marks, J.E.
Marlowe, Miss Clara S.

Plant, Chas.
Playford, James
Plumb, F.W.
Polito, Miss Marian
Polito, Sal
Polk, Kenneth
Pollock, Irwin
Poole, John A.
Poole, Wm. C.
Porter, W.R.
Postlewaite, Miss Mary A.
Potter, Miss Gail C.
Poupore, Mrs Judith
Powell, Mrs G.R.
Powell, Mrs H.C.
Power, Chas. N.
Powley, Mrs B.G.
Pratt, J. Ronald
Pratt, Mrs J.R.
Pratt, Michael
Prentice, Donald H.
Prentice, Martin W.
Prentice, Wm. B.
Presant, Fred W.
Preston, Dr Alan J.
Preston, Dr Helen A.
Pretty, David W.
Price, David E.
Prichard, Mrs J.S.
Prichard, Dr Sarah S.
Pringle, Mrs A.
Prychun, Miss Daria
Ptak, Dr W.T.
Ptak, Mrs W.T.
Pugh, Ronald R.
Pugsley, Robt. J.
Puglsey, Mrs R.J.
Purdy, David M.
Purdy, John B.
Purdy, Mrs J.B.
Purdy, Michael J.
Purry, P.S.
Purves, Norman W.
Puttock, Mrs Julie
Pybus, Mrs G.W.

Quesnell, Mrs M.

r

Radford, George
Radford, Mrs G.

Radford, Miss Mildred
Radley, Ronald L.
Rait, John S.
Ralbosky, Miss Elizabeth A.
Ralbosky, Joseph
Ramalho, Trevor
Ramphal, Dr Premdath J.
Ramsay, Wm. M.
Rankin, Mrs J.T.
Rankin, Wallace M.
Ranson, James A.
Ranson, Mrs J.A.
Raphael, Alan M.
Rawlins, Miss Bonnie
Rawlinson, Bruce A.
Rawlingson, Mrs B.A.
Rawson, Geo. H.
Rea, David E.
Reason, John W.
Redelmeier, Francis M.
Redner, Alan K.
Redner, John D.
Rees, Morgan V.A.
Rees, Mrs M.V.A.
Reeve, James M.
Reeve, Mrs J.M.
Reeves, H.A.
Reeves, Mrs H.A.
Reeves, Mrs L.A.
Reeves, Robert F.
Reeves, Mrs R.F.
Reeves, Robert L.
Regester, Michael P.S.D.
Reial, Dr Juri
Reial, Mrs J.
Reid, Donald A.
Reid, Mrs Ivor
Reid, Mrs J.E.
Reid, Mrs K.A.
Reid, Kevin C.
Reid, Martin F.
Reid, Robert
Reid, Mrs R.
Rendell, Mrs J.H.
Rentner, Mrs J.L.
Reynolds, George A.
Rice, Herb. F.
Rice, Mrs H.F.
Rich, Miss Louanne
Rich, Samuel L.
Rich, Mrs S.L.
Richards, John J.
Richards, W.M.
Rickards, John V.
Rickards, Mrs J.V.
Richardson, Geo. W.T.
Richardson, Ronald T.
Richardson, Mrs R.T.
Richardson, Wes. A.
Riddle, Robert J.
Riddle, Mrs R.J.
Riddle, Miss Janet
Ridge, Dr F.G.
Ridge, Mrs F.G.
Riley, David I.C.
Riley, John H.C.
Riley, Mrs J.H.C.

Riley, John H.K.
Riley, Robin M.K.
Rimmer, Richard W.
Rimmington, Alan E.
Rimmington, Mrs Catharine
Rober, Howard T.
Roberts, Ben. M.
Roberts, Daniel M.
Roberts, H.E.
Roberts, Jas. H.
Roberts, Mrs J.H.
Robertson, A.S.
Robertson, David J.
Robertson, Miss Elizabeth A.
Robertson, George M.
Robertson, Mrs J.G.
Robertson, Mrs J.M.
Robertson, Mrs K.
Robinsky, Mrs Evelyn G.
Robinson, Dr A.C.
Robinson, Mrs A.C.
Robinson, Derek J.
Robinson, Mrs D.
Robinson, Miss Kathleen J.
Robinson, Sidney H.
Robinson, Mrs S.H.
Robinson, Wm. A.
Robinson, Mrs W.A.
Robson, Mrs R.H.
Roche, John P.
Roche, Michael P.
Roche, P.M.
Rodgers, Mrs C.E.
Rodway, Douglas J.
Rodway, Dr John S.
Rodway, Spencer L.
Rogers, Guy W.
Rogers, Miss Josephine L.
Rogers, Roy P.
Rogers, Steven F.
Rohmer, Miss Ann M.
Rohmer, Miss Catherine O.
Rose, Miss Kathleen A.
Rosen, Dr Irving B.
Rosen, Mrs I.
Rosen, Michael
Rosen, Mrs M.
Rosen, Michael R.
Ross, Douglas C.
Ross, Mrs Elizabeth A.
Ross, Gary W.
Ross, Mrs J.L.
Ross, Peter
Ross, Mrs R.C.
Ross, Richard P.B.
Ross, Stephen G.
Ross, Victor
Rothbart, Dr Peter
Rothschild, M.J.
Rothwell, Miss Sarah A.
Roughton, Miss Heather
Row, Mrs W.S.
Rubens, Robert
Ruest, Ronald E.
Rutherford, Colin W.
Rutherford, Chris. H.
Rutherford, John M.

Rutherford, Robert T.
Rutherford, Mrs R.T.
Ruttonsha, Zareer S.
Rychlovsky, Miss Denise
Ryan, D.P.

S

Salloum, Peter A.
Salloum, Mrs P.A.
Sampson, Chas. W.J.
Samuel, Norman
Samuel, Mrs Norman
Samuels, Harvey E.
Samuels, Mrs H.E.
Samuels, Mrs H.R.
Samuels, Lawrence
Samuels, Mrs L.
Sanders, A.F.
Sanders, Mrs A.F.
Sands, A. Norman
Sanderson, Andrew
Sanderson, Miss Catherine A
Sanderson, Karl
Sanderson, Michael
Sarachman, W.P.
Sarachman, Mrs W.P.
Saul, Wilford G.R.
Saul, Mrs W.G.R.
Saunders, Guy
Saunders, Mrs G.
Saunders, Robt E.
Sawyer, Henry J.
Sawyer, Mrs H.J.
Sawyer, Miss Laura
Sawyer, Miss Maria
Sbrolla, Donald D.
Scace, Andrew C.
Scace, Mrs Arthur L.
Scace, Arthur R.A.
Scace, Mrs A.R.A.
Scandrett, Jas. H.H.
Schatz, Dr Douglas L.
Schatz, Mrs D.L.
Schultz, E.R.
Schultz, Harry L.
Schultz, Mrs H.L.
Schurman, Miss Laurie
Schurman, John N.
Schurman, Mrs J.N.
Schwill, Lothar B.
Sclater, Robert H.
Scott, Allan
Scott, Chris.
Scott, Mrs C.D.
Scott, Mrs E.S.
Scott, John G.B.
Scott, O.N.
Scott, Rex C.
Seagram, Robert D.
Seagram, N.O.
Sear, David J.
Seath, John
Sedgewick, Mrs C.N.

Sedgewick, Miss Eliz.
Seger, Dr Marianne
Seli, William K.
Semmons, Frank F.
Semple, Gordon C.
Severs, Mrs George
Seward, Dennis J.
Shanly, Ernest S.
Shanly, J.S.
Shapero, Dr Stephen E.
Sharpe, Mrs Alex. B.
Sharatt, Mrs L.D.
Sharpstone, Wm.
Shaver, Mrs George
Shaw, Andrew F.
Shaw, Douglas V.
Shaw, Mrs D.V.
Shaw, Ian
Shaw, John B.
Shaw, Ran. D.
Shaw, Mrs R.D.
Shedlowski, Richard W.
Sheedy, John B.
Sheedy, Mrs J.B.
Shelton, Mrs P.A.
Shenstone, Mrs P.
Sherk, Mrs D.
Shields, Miss Shelly
Shirreff, Bruce M.
Shirreff, Duncan J.
Shirt, John C.
Shortridge, Mrs K.
Shrubb, Wayne D.
Sifton, Mrs C.
Simmonds, Miss Catherine
Simmonds, Miss Joy
Simmonds, Monty M.
Simmonds, Mrs M.M.
Simms, Thomas B.
Simon, Mrs Rita
Simpkins, Arthur C.
Simpson, Mrs R.P.
Sims, Dr Stuart D.
Sims, Mrs S.D.
Simunek, Michael
Sinclair, Donald J.
Sinclair, Mrs D.J.
Sinclair, Mrs Eleanor
Sinclair, Prof. George
Sinclair, John G.
Sinclair, Joel G.
Sinclair, Mrs J.G.
Sinclair, Kenneth D.
Sinclair, Mrs K.D.
Sinclair, Miss Kathryn
Sissons, H.J.
Skinner, Henry A.P.
Skinner, Ross M.
Skuy, P.P.
Skuy, Percy
Skuy, Mrs P.
Slosiar, John G.
Small, Wm. W.
Smalley, F.M.
Smalley, Mrs F.M.
Smart, Mrs F.C.
Smart, Robert F.

Smith, Adam
Smith, Miss Amy I.
Smith, Miss Barbara J.
Smith, Mrs E.L.G.
Smith, Grant R.
Smith, Mrs G.R.
Smith, Miss Kathy
Smith, Kenneth R.
Smith, Mrs K. Raeburn
Smith, Stephen G.
Smith, Mrs W. Duncan
Smith, W. Jaffrey
Smith, Wm. J.
Smith, Mrs W.J.
Smith, Wm. K.
Smith, Mrs W.K.
Snell, Paul F.
Snelling, Mrs C.E.
Soame, E.J.
Soame, Mrs E.J.
Soanes, Dr Sidney V.
Soanes, Mrs S.V.
Soloninka, Harry
Soloninka, Mrs H.
Somerset, Mrs F.M.
Somerville, W.H.
Sparks, John D.
Sparks, Mrs J.D.
Sparling, Mrs E.A.
Spearing, Miss Arden
Spence, Miss Anne
Spence, Chas. S.
Spence, Mrs C.S.
Spence, Charles D.
Spence, George H.
Spero, J. Bruce
Spratt, Richard
Spratt, Mrs R.
Spriggs, Robert H.
Squires, Edward M.
Squires, Frank M.
Standen, Ms Gale
Standing, Robert M.
Standing, Mrs R.M.
Stanley, Mrs A.A.
Stanners, James E.
Stanners, Robert P.
Starnino, Mrs R.J.
Staroba, Mirek
Stauble, David R.
Stauble, Dr. W.J.
Stearns, Marshall
Stein, Mrs F.P.
Stephen, John G.
Stephen, Mrs J.G.
Stephenson, Donald J.G.
Stephenson, Mrs D.J.
Stephenson, John K.
Stephenson, Mrs J.K.
Stephenson, Mrs W.F.
Stevens, R.J.
Stevenson, Mrs J.D.
Stevenson, Mrs T.
Stewart, A.E.
Stewart, Mrs A.E.
Stewart, Alexander
Stewart, Mrs A.

Stewart, Dr D.A.
Stewart, Mrs D.A.
Stewart, Dr Donald A.
Stewart, F.W.D.
Stewart, James
Stewart, John H.
Stewart, Mrs M.D.
Stewart, Mrs Richard
Stimers, R.D.
Stock, Mrs Evelyn
Stone, Gregory
Stong, Louis J.
Stowe, Mrs W.W.
Strachan, Lorne D.
Straight, Beverley J.
Strain, Jas. T.
Strang, Mrs Maria
Stranks, Dr Gordon
Stranks, Mrs G.
Stranks, G. Murray
Stranks, Ian M.
Stranks, Kenneth A.
Stranks, Mrs K.A.
Stranks, Stuart L.
Strickland, Robert G.
Stripp, Mrs E.R.
Strong, Lawrence F.
Strong, Mrs L.F.
Stroud, Mrs V.G.
Struthers, James A.
Struthers, Mrs J.A.
Struthers, John A.
Sturdee, I.C.P.
Sturdee, Mrs I.C.P.
Suckling, Mrs Margaret
Suckling, Robert T.
Sugar, Mrs Helen
Sugar, Steven
Sugarman, Ms B.
Sullivan, E.C.
Sunter, Alex.
Sunter, Mrs A.
Suter, Robert H.
Suter, Mrs R.H.
Sutton, Edward E.
Sutton, Miss Susan H.
Suydam, John Rex
Swartz, Miss Mary Ann
Sydia, Robert W.
Sydia, Mrs R.W.
Sykes, Leon
Symes, Mrs P.G.
Symons, A.P.
Symons, John T.
Symons, Mrs J.T.
Szamos, Miss Cecelia
Szivek, John A.

t

-Pow, John

Tait, James R.
Tait, Mrs J.R.
Tasker, Miss Linda
Tattersall, John K.
Tattersall, Mrs J.K.
Tattle, John A.
Taylor, Miss Ann D.A.
Taylor, Miss Barbara
Taylor, Mrs Caley
Taylor, Douglas A.
Taylor, Mrs D.A.
Taylor, Douglas R.
Taylor, Miss Gail M.
Taylor, Mrs H.W.
Taylor, Jas. R.N.
Taylor, Kenneth M.
Taylor, Miss Lynda M.
Taylor, Dr M.M.
Taylor, Miss Margot
Taylor, Richard W.
Taylor, Mrs R.W.
Taylor, T.B.
Taylor, Mrs T.B.
Taylor, Vern
Taylor, Vincent
Taylorson, Nigel D.
Telfer, Adam A.
Terpenning, Miss Barbara
Terry, Miss Helen
Terry, Wm. C.
Tevlin, John D.
Tevlin, Thomas A.
Thickett, Francis G.
Thomas, Mrs A.D.
Thomas, Alan R.
Thomas, Mrs A.R.
Thomas, Mrs J.W.N.
Thomas, Peter
Thomas, Ronald H.
Thomas, Mrs R.H.
Thomas, Victor N.
Thomas, Mrs V.N.
Thompson, Alex D.
Thompson, Miss Elaine M.
Thompson, George A.
Thompson, Mrs G.A.
Thompson, Mrs Helen K.
Thompson, John W.
Thompson, Roderick
Thompson, Miss Virginia
Thomson, Garth
Thomson, Mrs M.C.
Thomson, Miss Marilyn
Thornback, Mrs Peter
Thornbury, Ronald W.
Thornbury, Mrs R.W.
Throop, Paul J.
Thurlow, Mrs R.C.
Tibbles, Miss Penny
Tiffany, Edward C.
Tiffany, Mrs E.C.
Till, F.L.
Till, Mrs F.L.
Timpson, Wm. S.
Timpson, Mrs W.S.
Tisdall, Mrs C.E.
Titus, Douglas G.

Titus, Mrs D.G.
Titus, Mrs R.W.
Topping, Alan P.
Topping, Mrs A.P.
Topping, Bryon
Townley, Miss Deborah A.
Townley, Mrs W.B.
Townshend-Carter, Philip A.G.
Trasiewicz, Julian
Trasiewicz, Mrs Lorie
Tremblay, Mrs Barbara A.
Trent, Gordon
Trevithick, John
Trim, Mrs J.D.
Trow, Wm. A.
Truemner, Wm. J.D.
Trumble, Richard
Trumper, R.A.
Trumper, Mrs R.A.
Tuck, John A.
Tuck, Mrs J.A.
Tuck, David R.
Tudhope, H.L.
Tyrwhitt, Philip
Tytler, Mrs Norman
Tytler, Miss Ruth

u

Udell, Frank E.K.
Usatis, Michael
Usatis, Wm. V.
Usatis, Mrs Wm. V.
Uuemae, Roger

v

Van de Meerendonk, Miss Rosemieke
Van Dalen, Mrs Heather
Vanderwal, Mrs D.
Van Patter, Hugh R.
Van Patter, Dr Hugh T.
Van Patter, Mrs H.T.
Van Reet, Hector
Van Reet, Mrs H.
Vanstone, Frank S.
Van'Thof, Johan
Varkony, Thomas J.
Varkony, Mrs T.J.
Vasoff, James D.
Vasoff, Mrs J.D.
Vaughan, Rev Dr Harold W.
Vaughan, Mrs J.
Vaughan, Kim
Von Buttlar, Stephen
Von Buttlar, Mrs S.
Vorps, Harry
Vorps, Robert
Vyoral, J.J.
Vyoral, Mrs J.J.

173

W

Wadham, A.E.
Wadham, Mrs A.E.
Wagdin, Vance
Wagner, Mrs James H.
Wahn, Gordon D.A.
Wahn, Ian G.
Wahn, Ian G.V.
Wainman, Dwight W.
Wainman, Mrs D.W.
Waisberg, Judge H.
Wait, Leonard R.
Wait, Mrs L.
Walford, Hugh C.
Wallace, Chas. R.
Walker, Denzil R.A.
Walker, Gerald N.
Walker, Miss Phyllis
Walsh, Brian Edward
Walters, Mrs B.
Walters, Walter
Walton, Miss Isobel J.
Walton, Miss Margaret A.
Wansbrough, Fred A.
Ward, Mrs David
Ward, Dr John F.
Ward, Mrs J.F.
Warden, W.G.J.
Warden, Mrs W.G.J.
Warren, F.A.
Wassif-Suleiman, Miss Erika
Watanabe, Mrs Junicki
Waterman, Harry J.
Waterman, Mrs H.J.
Watson, Miss Laurene
Watson, Neal M.
Watson, Mrs N.M.
Watson, Peter
Watson, Wilfred A.
Watson, Mrs W.A.
Watt, John A.
Watt, Wm. J.
Watt, Mrs W.J.
Waugh, Wm. G.
Webb, A.P.
Webber, Ross H.
Webber, Mrs R.
Webster, Alan N.
Webster, John D.
Wedgbury, John R.
Weigle, Douglas K.
Weir, Robert E.
Weir, Mrs Robert
Welch, John A.
Welch, Mrs J.A.
Wells, Mrs George
Wells, Stanley J.
Welsh, Miss Ann
Welsh, Mrs C.E.
Welsh, Miss Patricia
Welsh, Mrs Ruth

Welsh, Thomas
Welsh, Mrs T.
Welsh, Mrs W.K.
Westcott, Mrs B.B.
Westcott, Gregg
Weston, David
Weston, Mrs D.
Weston, W. Galen
Wheeler, Norman O.
Whibley, Mrs F.D.
Whipp, Harold H.
Whipp, Mrs H.H.
Whitaker, Patrick A.
Whitaker, Mrs P.A.
White, John K.
White, Mrs J.K.
White, Norman A.
White, Mrs N.A.
White, Mrs P.S.
Whittaker, Geo. G.
Whittaker, Mrs G.G.
Wiffen, Eric G.
Wighton, Eric A.A.
Wighton, Mrs E.A.A.
Wighton, Miss Lorna A.
Wigley, E.A.
Wilbee, Edward V.
Wilcox, Miss Mary
Wildbur, Geoffrey C.
Wiley, Mrs P.L.
Willcocks, Wm. G.
Willcocks, Mrs W.G.
Willett, Howard
Williams, Donald A.
Williams, E.A.
Williams, John H.C.
Williams, Owen S.
Williams, Wm. H.
Williamson, K.W.
Williamson, Mrs K.W.
Williamson, V.H.H.
Williamson, Mrs V.H.H.
Willis, Mrs Bruce C.
Willson, Mrs W.A.
Willson, Walter E.
Willson, Mrs W.E.
Wilson, Bryan Hugh
Wilson, C.W.
Wilson, Mrs C.W.
Wilson, Benson A.
Wilson, P.J.
Wilson, R.F.
Wilson, Dr Ronald H.
Wilson, T. B.
Wilson, Miss Vanessa C.
Wilson, W.F.
Wilson, Mrs W.F.
Wimmer, Frank
Winkler, Miss Rochelle
Winters, Jas. M.
Winters, Paul
Whittstock, Jeffrey
Wodzicki, Frank
Wodzicki, Peter A.
Wood, Mrs David
Wood, James D.
Wood, Mrs J.H.

Wood, J.H.M.
Wood, Miss Judi C.
Woods, Chris.
Woods, Mrs C.
Woolley, Fred C.
Woolley, Mrs F.C.
Woollcombe, Mrs E.M.
Wotherspoon, Richard H.
Wotherspoon, Mrs R.H.
Wray, Mrs J.W.
Wrigglesworth, Harold
Wright, Edward J.
Wright, Hugh D.
Wright, Mrs H.D.
Wulsin, Eugene,
Wulsin, Mrs E.
Wurtzburg, Chris. B.
Wyse, J.W.
Wyse, Mrs J.W.

Y

Yarker, Mrs John L.
Yatabe, Mrs M.
Yoerger, J.S.
Yoerger, Mrs J.S.
Yott, Robert J.
Youell, L.L.
Young, David
Young, Mrs Sandra
Young, Miss Deborah A.
Young, Donald A.
Young, Mrs Donald A.
Young, Gregory A.
Young, Mrs E.H.
Young, Mrs Helen
Young, Mrs James M.
Young, Mrs Shirley
Young, Miss Susan
Young, Mrs W.J.
Younker, Harry R.
Youseff, George M.
Youseff, Mrs G.M.
Youseff, Marcus
Yule, Miss Catharine

Z

Zachary, Mrs James P.
Zacher, Donald A.
Zacher, Mrs D.A.
Zachev, Michael
Zander, Herman P.
Zander, Mrs H.P.
Zeskoski, Dimitar
Zimmerman, Mrs H.A.
Zimmerman, Miss Karen M.

Books, periodicals

Adam, G.M. *Toronto Old and New.* Toronto, 1891.

Annual of the Ontario Branch of the Royal Caledonian Curling Club. Toronto, 1876-1932.

Bicket, James. *The Canadian Curler's Manual.* Toronto, 1840.

Bowen, Ronald. *Cricket: A History of its Growth and Development Throughout the World.* London, 1970.

Boyle, David. *The Township of Scarborough, 1766-1896.* 1896.

Britton, Charles J. *Cricket Books.* Birmingham, 1929.

The Canadian Cricketer's Guide. Ottawa, 1876.

Canadian Skater. Official publication of the Canadian Figure Skating Association.

Chadwick, Edward Marion. *Ontarian Families.* New Jersey, 1970.

Clark, S.D. *The Social Development of Canada.* Toronto, 1942.

Copleston, Mrs. Edward. *Canada: Why We Live in it and Why We Like it.* London, 1861.

Creelman, W.A. *Curling Past and Present.* Toronto, 1950.

Dickens, Charles. *American Notes and Pictures from Italy.* New York, 1905.

Dickson, George, and G. Adam Mercer. *A History of Upper Canada College.* Toronto 1893.

Easton, George. *Travels in America.* Edinburgh, 1871.

Edwards, Frederick. "Biggest Show on Ice." *Maclean's* 1 March 1938, vol. 51, no. 5., p. 40.

Firth, Edith G. *The Town of York, 1793-1815.* Toronto, 1962.

~ *The Town of York,* 1815-1834, Toronto. 1966.

Fitzgerald, R.A. *Wickets in the West.* London, 1873.

Goheen, Peter G. *Victorian Toronto, 1850-1900: Patterns of Growth.* Chicago, 1970.

Goodfellow, Arthur R. *Wonderful World of Skates.* USA, 1972.

A Guide to the John Ross Robertson Canadian Historical Collection in the Toronto Public Library, Landmarks of Canada, 1967.

Guillet, Edwin C. *Toronto: From Trading Post to Great City.* Toronto, 1934.

~ *Pioneer Inns and Taverns.* Toronto, 1954.

Hall, John E., and R.O. McCullough. *Sixty Years of Canadian Cricket.* Toronto, 1895.

Heathcote, J.M., and C.G. Tebbutt. *Skating,* and Witham, T. Maxwell. *Figure Skating.* London, 1909. Two volumes bound as one, sharing a single title page.

Heyes, Esther. *Etobicoke, From Furrow to Borough.* Etobicoke, Ontario, 1974.

Howell, Nancy, and Maxwell Howell. *Sports and Games in Canadian Life: 1700 to the Present.* Toronto, 1969.

Kalman, Harold. *Pioneer Churches.* Toronto, 1976.

Kerr, John. *Curling in Canada and the United States.* Edinburgh, 1904.

Lamb, W. Kaye. *Canada's Five Centuries.* Toronto, 1971.

Lindsey, G.G.S., and D.W. Saunders. *Cricket across the Sea.* Toronto, 1887.

Lovell, John (ed.). *80 Years' Progress in British North America.* 1863.

[MacLean, John S.?] *Toronto Skating Club* (1895-1942). Unpublished manuscript included in Toronto Skating Club papers on deposit with Metropolitan Toronto Central Library.

Marder, John I. *The International Series.* London, 1968.

McNaught, Kenneth. *The Pelican History of Canada.* Harmondsworth, England, 1969.

Meagher, George. *Lessons in Skating.* New York, 1900.

Middleton, Jesse Edgar. *The Municipality of Toronto—A History.* 3 vols. Toronto, 1923.

~ *Toronto's 100 Years.* Toronto, 1934.

Morrison, John T. *A History of the Toronto Skating Club from its inception in 1895 until its Amalgamation with the Toronto Cricket Club and the Victoria Club in 1957 to Form the Present Day Toronto Cricket, Skating and Curling Club.* Unpublished manuscript included in Toronto Skating Club papers on deposit with Metropolitan Toronto Central Library. 1975.

Reed, T.A. *The Blue and White: A record of Fifty Years of Athletic Endeavour at the University of Toronto.* Toronto, 1944.

Rubenstein, Louis. *Skating in Canada.* London, 1888.

St Catharines Cricket Club. *Canadian Cricketer's Guide.* St Catharines. Canada West, 1858.

Sayen, Henry. *A Yankee Looks at Cricket.* London, 1956.

Scadding, Henry. *Toronto of Old.* Toronto, 1873.

Sheppard, John. *Cricket: More than a Game.* London, 1975.

Smith, D.W. Various unpublished papers on deposit with Metropolitan Toronto Central Library.

Toronto Cricket, Skating and Curling Club. Papers, 1919-1970. On deposit with Metropolitan Toronto Central Library.

Toronto Skating Club, *Carnival Programme, 1930-56.* Toronto.

Weld, Charles Richard. *A Vacation Tour in the United States and Canada.* London, 1855.

Wise, S.F., and Douglas Fisher. *Canada's Sporting Heroes.* Don Mills, Ontario, 1974.

Withrow, Rev. William H. *A Popular History of the Dominion of Canada.* Toronto, 1884.

Newspapers

Canadian Freeman,
York

Colonial Advocate,
Queenston and York

Daily Mail and Empire,
Toronto

Examiner,
Toronto

Globe and Mail,
Toronto

Patriot,
Toronto

Toronto *Daily Star,*
Toronto

Toronto *Herald,*
Toronto

Toronto *Mail,*
Toronto

PICTURE CREDITS

The drawings, paintings, and photographs which illustrate the "ancient" history of the TCSCC in this book have been obtained, in large part, from the public collections of three large archives – the Public Archives of Canada (abbreviated as PAC in the credits which follow), the Metropolitan Toronto Library Board (MTLB), and the Ontario Archives (OA). The balance of the historical material has been loaned by the club and club members for inclusion in the book. The publisher has made all reasonable efforts to establish copyright in the borrowed material and apologizes for those names he has omitted through ignorance. The photographic essay by John de Visser (JDV) on pages 143-158 was produced during the last week of 1976.

ABC News Pictures: 134 / Ashley & Crippen: 114 (*bottom*) / Brantford *Expositor:* 138 (*bottom*) / E. Bratton: 105 / Stanley Fillmore: 38 / *Globe & Mail:* 136 (*top left*) / Holiday Studio: 95; 96 / Leonardi: 95 / H.H. Menzies: 87 (*top*) / MTLB: 19; 36; 37; 41; 48; 50; 51; 66; 67; 74 (*bottom*); 76; 82; 83; 98-100; 103; 131 / Gilbert A. Milne: 138 (*top left & right*) / D. Newman: 114 (*top*) / R.A. Nicholls: 89 / OA: 44; 81; 85; 122 / PAC: 17; 18; 20; 21; 22-24; 26-32; 34; 40; 43; 64; 71; 72; 74 (*top*); 121; 125; 126; 132; 133 / Norman Seagram: 54 (*bottom*); 140; 141 (*top*) / Toronto *Star:* 54 (*centre*) / Toronto *Star Weekly:* 52; 53 / Toronto *Telegram:* 54 (*top*); 136 (*bottom right*) / G.E.P. Tuck: 58 / TCSCC: 25; 47; 55 (*top*); 106; 107; 117 (*lower left & centre*); 128; 129 / JDV: 130; 141 (*bottom*); 143-158; 160.